Wilhelm Cramer, John Peter M. Schleuter

The Christian Mother, the Education of her Children and her Prayer

Wilhelm Cramer, John Peter M. Schleuter

The Christian Mother, the Education of her Children and her Prayer

ISBN/EAN: 9783337791353

Printed in Europe, USA, Canada, Australia, Japan

Cover: Foto ©Lupo / pixelio.de

More available books at **www.hansebooks.com**

THE
Christian Mother.

THE EDUCATION OF HER CHILDREN,
AND
HER PRAYER.

From the German of REV. W. CRAMER.
Translated by a Father of the Society of Jesus, with the permission of Superiors.

WITH AN INTRODUCTION
BY
MOST REV. JAMES GIBBONS, D.D.,
Archbishop of Baltimore.

Twentieth Thousand.

NEW YORK, CINCINNATI, AND ST. LOUIS:
Benziger Brothers,
PRINTERS TO THE HOLY APOSTOLIC SEE.

𝔍𝔪𝔭𝔯𝔦𝔪𝔞𝔱𝔲𝔯,

† JAMES GIBBONS,

Archbishop of Baltimore.

𝔍𝔪𝔭𝔯𝔦𝔪𝔞𝔱𝔲𝔯,

JOHN, CARDINAL MCCLOSKEY,

Archbishop of New York.

COPYRIGHT, 1880, BY BENZIGER BROTHERS.

APPROBATIONS TO
THE CHRISTIAN MOTHER.

CINCINNATI, Aug. 16, 1880.

I wish very much you would take measures to circulate as widely as possible the book called THE CHRISTIAN MOTHER. I have not had time to read it all, but the portions I have read, in various parts of the book, have so impressed me that I do not know of any new book I have seen of late years calculated to do more efficient and wide-spread good through the country. I wish that every mother in the land would study it and profit by it.

Your servant in Christ,

✠ WILLIAM HENRY ELDER,
Coadjutor Bishop.

LITTLE ROCK, Ark., July 24, 1880.

Please send me twelve copies of THE CHRISTIAN MOTHER. . . . . I regard the book as a very useful and instructive little publication. Yours faithfully,

✠ EDWARD FITZGERALD,
Bishop of Little Rock.

ERIE, July 17, 1880.

As yet I have read but a few chapters of THE CHRISTIAN MOTHER, recently published by you. Yet I have read enough to convince me that the book is admirably adapted to the wants of our age, and eminently calculated to promote the cause of Christian morality. The mere perusal of the Chapter on the Mother of a Priest would convince any Catholic at least that I have not exaggerated the merits of the work. Yours sincerely,

✠ T. MULLEN,
Bishop of Erie.

BUFFALO, July 22, 1880.

I beg thankfully to acknowledge your little book THE CHRISTIAN MOTHER. It is an admirable little book; would to God that every young mother in the land had a copy, read a chapter of it daily, and followed its directions in her own life and in the education of her children. No better present could the zealous pastor give the young woman on the eve of her marriage than this same CHRISTIAN MOTHER. Yours very truly,

✠ S. V. RYAN,
Bishop of Buffalo.

Approbations to the CHRISTIAN MOTHER.

Paper, 25 cts., maroquette, full gilt side, 35 cts.; cloth, 50 cts.; French mor., flex., red edges, $1.00.

TORONTO, Aug. 19, 1880.

I had to stop the reading from time to time to utter a strong prayer to our good God, that every mother could have a copy of the book.

✠ JOHN JOSEPH LYNCH,
Archbishop of Toronto.

ST. PAUL, Oct. 28, 1880.

Could every mother be induced to put in practice the lessons of this book, what blessings would thence derive to themselves, to their children, and to society!

✠ THOMAS L. GRACE,
Bishop of St. Paul.

MARYSVILLE, All Souls' Day, 1880.

* * * The study of the "Christian Mother" would be a great help to many a mother, in the work of their own sanctification, as well as in the education of their children.

✠ E. O'CONNELL,
Bishop of Grass Valley.

TUAM, Oct. 28, 1880.

* * * It possesses the great advantage of being very practical, as it proposes nothing extraordinary, nothing to interfere with the ordinary discharge of parents' domestic and family duties. * * *

✠ JOHN MacEVILLY,
Bishop of Galway and Coadjutor of Tuam.

MARQUETTE, Mich., Sept. 22, 1880.

The little book should be introduced into every Catholic family, for the instruction of parents as well as children, wherefore we earnestly recommend it.

✠ JOHN VERTIN,
Bishop of Marquette.

VANCOUVER, W. T., Sept. 29, 1880.

I am well pleased with it, and would like to see it in the hands of every Christian mother. * * *

✠ ÆGIDIUS JUNGER,
Bishop of Nesqually.

BENZIGER BROTHERS, New York, Cincinnati, and St. Louis.

The Catholic Press on "The Christian Mother."

This beautiful little book breathes forth a most consoling piety from every page.—*Boston Pilot.*

This beautiful little book directs the mother in all her Christian duties. It is a guide in her ministry of love, care, and education to her children.—*Waterloo Catholic Times.*

A most admirable little manual of instruction and devotion. It contains devotions and instructions for every relation in which the Christian mother may be placed, and as her daily companion in all the trying circumstances to which she may be exposed, it has the means of consolation ready in a resort to its pages.—*Toronto Tribune.*

Every mother should possess a copy of this charming little work, for it is not large, but truly it contains *multum in parvo.*—*N. Y. Tablet.*

This excellent little work, which is both a book of instruction and one of prayer, should be in the hands of every Christian mother, for in its pages will be found all those helps which religion gives in the responsible duties of a mother's life.—*New Orleans Morning Star.*

Gives most salutary counsel on the education of children.—*New England Catholic Herald.*

Devotional, instructive, and a practical guide for the mother of a family who delights in the sanctification of herself and her children.—*Parkersburg Catholic Messenger.*

We ask for it a careful perusal on the part of mothers. —*Pittsburg Catholic.*

We cannot recommend this book too strongly, and we would be pleased to see it in every Catholic home.— *Kansas City Catholic Banner.*

It is full of the most useful instruction to Christian mothers, and should have a wide circulation.—*North-Western Chronicle.*

BENZIGER BROTHERS, New York, Cincinnati, and St. Louis.

The Catholic Press on "The Christian Mother."

We have never seen so complete and beautiful a religious manual for Christian Mothers. It wants nothing but to be well used.—*London Tablet*.

* * * It would be well if all mothers were deeply conscious of the lofty trust committed to their hands and proportionately faithful in its discharge. This little book is designed to remind them of their many duties or concurrent parts of one great duty, and to afford them help and counsel how best to perform them. The author lays down vividly, and with not unnecessary plainness, the many difficulties that beset a proper Christian education of the young, owing to the many dangers by which childhood is environed from the very cradle, the negligence, excessive indulgence, and too often the bad example of parents, and gives some wholesome admonitions on these and other points. There are in the end some excellent prayers and pious practices for Christian mothers, amongst others a useful method of assisting at the Holy Sacrifice for their own benefit and that of their children.—*The American Catholic Quarterly Review*.

A book for mothers, a book full of sweetness and light, a book abounding in wise counsels, ennobling thoughts, and efficacious prayers, a book most opportune and useful for the women of this day and this land, a book coming from a priestly heart, a book beautiful. With great goodwill we commend it to those for whom it was written.—*The Catholic Mirror*.

The work is one which every mother can use with great spiritual advantage, and might well be a *vade mecum* to everyone who desires to train her children in the ways of true religion.—*Catholic Standard*.

It should find its way into every Catholic household, and into every Catholic mother's hand, and its teachings to her heart.—*Buffalo Catholic Union*.

BENZIGER BROTHERS, New York, Cincinnati, and St. Louis.

CONTENTS.

PART I.

	PAGE
The mother's first visit to church	5
Vocation and education of a mother	17
Necessary conditions	28
Fear of God and piety	31
Love for her children	40
The mother's dowry	54
The mother's consecration	63
The child's introduction into the truths of our holy religion	69
Proceedings against the child's faults	79
The guard of holy innocence	95
The mother's direction of her children	106
God's word to the Christian mother	124
The mother of a priest	129
The mother in her prayer	145

PART II.

Prayer on the anniversary-day of her marriage	157
Prayer for the first visit to church	160
Prayer in the morning	162
Prayer in the evening	163
Prayer at holy mass:	
For herself	165
For the benefit of her children	170

DIFFERENT PRAYERS FOR THE USE OF THE CHRISTIAN MOTHER.

For Herself:

To obtain the grace to give good example	175
To obtain true supernatural love for her children	176
To obtain true wisdom	178
For the gift of fortitude	180
For the spirit of mildness	181
To Jesus, the friend of children	182
To the Holy Ghost for His seven gifts	184
To the blessed Virgin Mary	186

CONTENTS.

	PAGE
To Saint Joseph	187
To the Guardian Angels	187
To the Saints whose names the children bear	188

For the Children:

- To obtain God's blessing on the labor she undergoes for her children ... 189
- For protection in all dangers ... 190
- That the Lord may preserve them from grievous sin ... 191
- To obtain for them the grace of the true fear of God ... 192
- To obtain for them the grace to fulfil the duties of their state of life ... 193
- To obtain for them the virtue of chastity ... 194
- To obtain for them a true love of their neighbor ... 195
- To obtain for them the love of truth ... 196
- For the children when frequenting school ... 196
- For the children when preparing for first confession ... 197
- For the children when preparing for their first holy communion ... 198
- That God may dispose for the best the temporal affairs of the child ... 200
- To be said for children who are addicted to certain faults ... 201
- To obtain for children the seven gifts of the Holy Ghost ... 203

Devotion of the Holy Way of the Cross ... 205
The Rosary of a mother ... 219
Prayers at confession ... 222
Prayers at holy communion ... 226
Prayer of a mother for her husband ... 229
Prayer to obtain the chastity of her state of life ... 230
Prayer of a mother when with child ... 233
Prayer to obtain for her son vocation to the priesthood ... 234
Prayer to be said for a son who has a vocation for the priesthood ... 236
Litany of the Christian mother ... 238
Prayer to the Sacred Heart of Jesus ... 249
Prayers to be said in common with the children:
- Morning prayers ... 251
- Evening prayers ... 253
- When taking Holy Water before retiring ... 255
- Before meals ... 255
- After meals ... 255

INTRODUCTION.

THE Christian mother has been charged by God with a two-fold mission with respect to her children; namely, the securing to them the nourishment of both soul and body. For if she has been fitted by Nature to give to her children the milk which sustains the life of their bodies, so likewise has she been peculiarly designed by the God of Nature to dispense to them for the nourishment of their souls the *rational milk* of which the apostle* speaks, and which will make them *grow unto salvation.*

Nor is this latter responsibility less imperative than the former. If she would consider herself derelict of duty to leave her offspring without the nourishment which sustains their natural and temporal life, still more guilty would she be were she to deprive them of the nourishment which will insure their supernatural and eternal life.

And how admirably is she not fitted for this latter mission, of the two the more important and more noble! She is by excellence the teacher of her children. Now we all know that much of the progress of a pupil depends not only on his natural gifts and talents, but also on the degree of confidence inspired by his teacher. But who shares the affection and confidence of the child like the mother? Does he not believe

*1 St. Peter i. 1, 2.

every word she says? And how firmly, therefore, and how deeply may not the Christian mother instil into his young mind those religious truths which will ever remain a pure and wholesome nourishment for his soul, giving it strength to reject the poison of unbelief so temptingly offered to it at some later day.

And if the mother be a true Christian—if she show forth in her own life the habit of the virtues which she desires to instil into the hearts of her children—how nobly and how successfully will she fulfil her mission!

The child is by nature an *imitator*. If the model set before him is good, there is reason to hope that the copy will be so likewise. Do mothers realize this? And when later in life they fail to see in their children the Christian virtues of humility, patience, charity, and forgiveness, do they not also fail to trace the absence of these virtues to its true and legitimate cause?

Oh! that all mothers would bear in mind that if they desire their children to become true Christians they must present in their own lives the models of which the children will be the living copies.

The object of this little book is to procure this result. May God bless the Christian mothers who read it and profit by it!

JAMES GIBBONS,
Archbishop of Baltimore.

Feast of St. Callistus, 1880.

PART I.

THE CHRISTIAN MOTHER.

The Education of her Children.

The Christian Mother.

THE MOTHER'S FIRST VISIT TO CHURCH.

THE present age, which in many respects has renounced God and religion, that is to say, the truth, no longer knows the true destiny of man, and gives itself up to the vain and erroneous belief, that he most perfectly attains the end of his existence, who secures for himself the greatest amount of earthly goods, worldly honors, and sensual pleasures. The Church, on the contrary, and the truth confided to her care, teach and proclaim that the end of our existence here upon earth, and of the existence of all created things, is the glorification of God and the salvation of man ; that we must live the life of the children of God, and by serving and glorifying Him make ourselves worthy of being admitted to the never-ending happiness of heaven. This also holds good with regard to the state of matrimony. The chief endeavors of married people must be directed towards serving God in the state of life on which they have entered, that in so doing they may work out the salvation of their immortal souls. But their special care must be for the children whom God may confide to them, to make them good and fervent Christians, who will prefer the service of God and the salvation of their souls to all things else.

It is for this reason that the Church does not allow her children to live in the state of matrimony before having offered to them a careful preparation—that is to say, before having first sanctified and consecrated them by that Holy Sacrament which our Divine Saviour Himself has for that purpose instituted and left to her care. By virtue of this Sacrament man and wife become in a mysterious manner intimately united, as Christ is united with His Church, so that they cease, as it were, to be two persons; "they shall be two in one flesh." All the graces they may stand in need of will through this Sacrament descend immediately upon the newly married couple, and continue to descend, enabling them to persevere in leading a truly Christian life, far different from that of the heathen, "who do not know God," but like to that which is expected of the "children of the Saints."

Wedlock thus consecrated and sanctified is blessed by the Lord;—the spouse becomes a mother. Rejoicing as a mother she holds her new-born babe in her arms. The word of the Lord has been verified in her: "A woman, when she is in labor, hath sorrow, because her hour is come; but when she hath brought forth the child, she remembereth no more the anguish, for joy that a man is born into the world" (St. John xvi.). But her joy is to become yet fuller.

The Church hastens to meet her and receives the child from her arms, in order that, after being freed by the waters of regeneration from the unenviable inheritance of our first parents, it may become a child of God. As such it is again confided to the happy mother, who, whilst casting the eye of faith on her darling, beholds henceforward also a child of God, clothed with all the majesty becoming the child of so great a Father, loved by Him even more than by herself, and endowed with the right, as honorable as it is unmerited, to become in due time an heir of God's own heavenly glory and happiness.

Is not this well calculated to fill a mother's heart, if enlightened by faith, with transports of joy and delight?

And what shall I say of her vocation from this day? What more precious in the sight of God than a child in whom is reflected the image of His divine majesty! This most precious gift He confides to the father, it is true, but especially to the mother, that henceforward she may be His helpmate in the grand work of fitting it for the enjoyment of heaven, for that glorious and blissful life which He has destined for it from all eternity, and that she may participate in that joy which is found in the consciousness of having worked for a soul's salvation.

What a glorious and high vocation! And consequently, what a high dignity is conferred on her—the dignity of a mother!

Behold here how we are to regard a Christian spouse after she becomes a mother! Will not, or rather must not, a grateful joy take possession of her heart? Will not the consciousness of her dignity as a mother, and of the consequent high and important duties devolving upon her, elevate her heart and at the same time urge it forward to a holy earnestness?

And when, after having endured the pangs of childbirth, she is again enabled and allowed to enter the house of God, what is more natural than that this her first visit to church should be made in an unusual manner, accompanied by a certain degree of solemnity? When again entering the house of Him who has heaped upon her so many favors and graces, will not her heart beat with new and increased feelings of gratitude, and will not these uncommon sentiments make her burst forth with greater fervor than ever in words of praise? Will not the remembrance of her motherhood and its duties become more lively and urge her to lay on the steps of the altar, in the sight of the Lord, the sacred vow to discharge henceforward conscientiously and faithfully all the duties of her vocation? And how appropriate is it to commend here, on this sacred spot, with renewed and increased fervor, sincerity, and confidence, the darling of her heart to the Lord and to His holy Mother, and to call down God's grace upon herself, upon her vocation, and upon all that will be henceforward incumbent upon her in the discharge of the difficult work of the education of her children?

These are the impressions and sentiments which are most naturally found in the heart of a truly Christian mother when making her first visit to church. But the Church, which delights in assisting her children in whatever regards their spiritual welfare and the promotion of their pious endeavors, proving herself thereby to be the divinely enlightened and highly privileged mother of all, has not been wanting in offering aid also to the Christian mother at this hallowed hour of life. In the person of the priest she joins the mother's company, that she may thus make her first visit to God's temple, led as it were by the hand of the Church, and prepared to perform the sacred ceremony in a manner more pleasing to God and more beneficial to herself.

At the entrance of the house of God the mother is met by the priest, vested with surplice and stole. The Church, keeping her eyes fixed only on the dignity and the high vocation upon which the mother has entered, welcomes her now with the pious wish that God's grace may be given to her, to enable her to live henceforward in a manner worthy of her vocation. The Church does this when she prays that God may sprinkle the mother with the dew of heavenly grace, whilst she is sprinkled with holy water, as if she wished to say: "As the drops of water blessed by me, which resemble drops of dew, fall on thee, so may also God's grace, like a refreshing dew, descend to strengthen thee in thy vocation." After this,—constantly keeping in view the dignity of a mother,—the Church places a burning candle in one of her hands, to remind her that she must let the light of Christian faith and of a truly Christian life so shine before her child that it "may see her good works," and, by imitating her, praise the Father in heaven. In the other hand is laid the end of the stole, to signify that she is willing now and during the whole time she will spend in her child's education to remain intimately united to the Church. It is in such close union with holy Church as this that the mother begins this her first visit to the house of God, and performs all these pious exercises. The priest therefore, whilst offering to her the stole, says: "Come into the temple of God, adore the Son of the blessed Virgin Mary, who has given to thee to be fruitful in thy offspring."

And in the lessons and prayers which the Church now orders the priest to recite in the mother's name, who in the meantime approaches the altar, three things, which are justly supposed to be found on such an occasion in a mother's heart, are expressed over and over again, viz., thanks for the divine favor bestowed on her, the resolution to educate the child in a Christian manner, and the petition for the divine assistance needed to do this.

After a psalm has been recited, the desires of the mother find expression in the "Our Father," in which she joins the priest, saying it devoutly not only in her own but also in her child's name. "Our Father," my Father and Father of my child; "hallowed be Thy name;" be Thou praised for all the favors and graces which Thou hast bestowed on me by the birth of a child and by its regeneration. May Thy holy name become henceforward through me and through my child constantly praised, blessed, and glorified. Grant this through Thy grace! "Thy kingdom come;" grant, Father, to me and to my child that we may both always and fully participate in the blessings of Thy holy Church and become thus more and more her worthy members. "Thy will be done," always and everywhere, in me and in my child, and also by me and by my child. "Give us our daily bread;" give and ordain all temporal things for my good and that of my child. "Forgive" whatever wrong I have committed until now. "Lead us," me and my child, "not into temptation, but deliver us from evil. Amen."

The "Our Father" is followed by the following responsive prayer, by which the Church implores God to pour out His treasures of grace upon the mother, that she may become enabled to fulfil all her duties:

Priest. "Save Thy handmaid, O Lord."

Server. "Trusting in Thee, O my Lord."

P. "Send her help, O Lord, from Thy sanctuary."

S. "And defend her from Sion."

P. "Let not the enemy have any power over her."

S. "Nor the son of iniquity presume to hurt her."

P. "O Lord, hear my prayer."
S. "And let my cry come unto Thee."
P. "The Lord be with thee."
S. "And with thy spirit."

LET US PRAY.

"Almighty, everlasting God, who, through the delivery of the blessed Virgin Mary, hast turned into joy the pains of the faithful in childbirth, look mercifully upon this Thine handmaid, coming in gladness to Thy temple, to offer up her thanks: and grant that, after this life, by the merits and intercession of the same blessed Mary, she may merit to arrive, together with her offspring, at the joys of everlasting happiness. Through Christ our Lord. R. Amen."

What an excellent prayer!

"By the birth of Jesus the pains of those who give birth to a child are turned into joy," since those who have been born into this world are now born again to be children of God, and thus to be the richest heirs of the Heavenly Father. Without being born again spiritually, the mere natural birth of a child would only be a cause of sorrow and mourning. "Coming in gladness to Thy temple to offer up her thanks." With gladness, we have heard the many reasons why there should be gladness "to offer up her thanks" for them; this is another reason why the mother goes to church on this day: "Grant that after this life," through the perfect fulfilment of her duties as a mother, educating her children in the fear of God and piety, "she may merit to arrive together with her offspring at the joys of everlasting happiness," just as she has been admitted to-day into Thy temple on earth, "full of joy," and that thus also her child, like her and through her, may be happy for all eternity.

After this the priest sprinkles her once more with holy water, in the form of a cross, saying: "May the peace and blessing of Almighty God the Father, the Son, and the Holy Ghost come down upon thee and remain with thee for ever. Amen." A blessing, indeed, full of real meaning, through which the Church asks for the mother and gives to her our Lord's gracious help, that she may be enabled to sanctify her vocation by fulfilling God's holy will, by honoring God, and by laboring for the child's true welfare.

Thus, then, the Church dismisses the

mother after having, as it were, consecrated, blessed, and enriched her with graces for the duties of that high and important vocation which she has to fulfil towards her child. In fact, the whole act of thus going again to the temple of God is a solemn introduction of the mother into her vocation, made at the hand of the Church. As we have already intimated, this occasion is to be improved, it is true, by acts of solemn thanksgiving; but the *vocation of a mother* is that upon which the Church lays the most stress. The mother must — this is the will of the Church—become conscious on this occasion of her high calling, and of the important duties of a mother. She is expected to recommend herself and her child, and all that she will have to do with regard to it, to the Lord. She is to be introduced into this important work by the Church and made strong by her blessing, and at her hand she must henceforth perform all her duties as a mother. How much, therefore, is it to be lamented that this beautiful act is so much neglected by Christian mothers! Is not neglecting it the same as withholding from themselves and from their children the blessings of the Church, and as robbing themselves of the highly salutary effect of this edifying ceremony? Would to God that this beautiful custom were to become again of universal practice! May all mothers perform it in the manner and with the sentiments we have pointed out! It would certainly be a great blessing for both mothers and children.

THE VOCATION AND EDUCATION OF A MOTHER.

As we have seen, the Church looks upon the vocation of a Christian mother as a thing of the greatest importance. This is the reason she introduces her with prayer and blessing into the house of God when she makes her first visit to it after her delivery. From that time she is called, in the name and place of the Church, to assist her child, her tender boy or girl, in obtaining that happiness which Christ has prepared for it, and must therefore, first of all, lead it to the practice of piety and of the fear of God. What the ministers of the Church do with regard to grown persons the mother must, according to circumstances, do with regard to her children during their childhood; becoming thus in truth a minister of holy Church. O sublime vocation! Let us look somewhat closer at it.

With regard to the child's natural life, it is during its first years exclusively dependent upon the mother. Its organs are still too tender to take nourishment directly from nature's hand. The mother therefore, according to the wise provision of our Creator, first receives the nourishment intended for the child, and only after it has become fit for its tender life, by the operations of the organs of her own body, she offers it to her offspring. And thus the child thrives bodily and grows, as it were, in its mother's arms and at its mother's breast.

But the little one has received still another life in holy baptism—the supernatural life of sanctifying grace, by which it has become a child of God. Now, as the Lord has deposited nourishment for the natural life in the world, so He has deposited nourishment for the supernatural life chiefly in His holy Church. The Church feeds and promotes this supernatural life by her doctrine, by her sacraments and other means of grace, and by her direction. But this she does, as long as the child's supernatural life is still tender and undeveloped, not directly, but by means of the mother. Neither is the child capable of receiving directly what is for the increase and growth of its supernatural life—that is to say, what is given to the Church for rearing it in piety and the fear of God. This must be prepared for it by its mother in a manner suited to its tender age. The mother must propose to the child sacred truths, practices and the virtues of a Christian life, in a childlike, simple, condescending manner, as if she were offering to it nourishing milk. In this sense, too, the child must in its earlier years rest, as it were, on the spiritual breast of its mother, and, in what regards the life of its soul, there it must grow and become strong.

In fact, the mother holds during her child's infancy, in the full sense of the word, the place of the Church. The command which is given by our Lord to His Church to help man to obtain his salvation, and consequently to implant in him Christian piety and the fear of God, must during his first and most tender years almost exclusively be fulfilled by the Christian mother. The Christian mother is the minister of the Church with regard to her child. Woe to her if she be ignorant or unmindful of this duty!

There is little hope that he will ever become a genuine and fervent Christian whose mother has neglected to inspire him in his infancy with a truly Christian spirit. As, generally speaking, no one comes into the possession of the blessings prepared for him by Christ unless they are offered to him by the Church, so we also remain, for the most part, more or less deprived of them if our mothers neglect to make us acquainted with them when we are still young.

But happy the child that enjoys the care of a mother who, animated with that true spirit which should be the life of every Christian, is both able and anxious to breathe this spirit into her children from their very infancy, and to lead them to practise all kinds of Christian virtues. It is almost certain that, at a subsequent period of life, the edifice of a Christian life will rise very high upon such a foundation laid by such a mother; that the child will grow up a good Christian, and will arrive one day at the haven of eternal happiness. How great is the number of saints who owe their wonderful sanctity and the high degree of their happiness in heaven, next to God, to the salutary influence of a pious mother! Yes, how many among the saints had saints for their mothers—a most important cause of their own sanctity! What a blessing, therefore, for the child to have a truly Christian, truly pious mother!

Again, the Christian mother is the servant of the Church with regard to her children. If she fulfils her duties faithfully, blessings will go out from her to the child, and to society at large. This is the reason why the Church takes all possible care to have the mother educated in a truly Christian manner. Since God Himself has given to the mother so high and important a vocation, He wished also to make her fit to discharge its duties perfectly. This is the reason why He has endowed females with a certain natural disposition for piety and for the practice of all those virtues which are essential to the right treatment and education of tender children. According to His wise dispositions, during those years when the child's heart is most susceptible to impressions made by grown persons, it lives almost exclusively under the eyes of the mother, who is often for whole days its only companion, whilst the father is attending to his business. It is also for this reason that it is so necessary for the mother's influence to be good, and for her to be animated with the spirit of the true fear of God and of piety. Such natural disposition given by God to females renders easy the exercise of piety and of those virtues which are necessary for a mother. Woe, therefore, yes, woe to a mother if she should be wanting in them!

Great also is the endeavor of the Church to educate truly Christian mothers. Who does not know the numerous institutions, societies, communities, founded within her for the benefit of youth, to preserve in them a truly Christian spirit, and especially to shelter them from the dangers that beset their innocence? And holy Church has in view above all the training of virgins for the vocation which most of them will follow, the vocation of a mother. She is anxious to educate truly Christian mothers.

Hence her great watchfulness and care when the first step towards this highly important vocation is taken, viz., when the virgin becomes a spouse. Ah, the danger of suffering shipwreck of that most precious good and ornament, her innocence, has perhaps now become far greater than ever. The Church knows perfectly well how great a misfortune it is when a virgin abuses the state of a bride by levity and dissoluteness. She knows the bride is suffering the loss of her most precious treasure in the loss of her innocence. How could the Church expect to see such a person become a truly good mother, in whom unfortunately together with innocence of heart and life other Christian virtues are likely to become impaired and gradually to disappear! Hence the great earnestness manifested in her exhortations and admonitions, in her warnings from the pulpit by the voice of the priest, in the confessional, and wherever occasion offers. Hence her recourse to so many means of all kinds to preserve her brides in purity and innocence of heart for their approach to the altar. If her holy endeavors are crowned with success, then they will become

—this is her joyous confidence—one day good and faithful mothers. May we not, in the levity with which those behave who are already engaged to enter the state of matrimony, find the cause why so many families exhibit such sad pictures of human misery, and why the duties of parents are so much neglected therein?

The momentous hour when the virgin is to become a wife draws near. It is therefore with motherly care that the Church approaches her, leaving nothing undone, in order that this important step may be taken with the most conscientious preparation. She has made it the duty of priests to cause bride and bridegroom to appear before them for the purpose of inducing both to begin an earnest preparation, and to give them at the same time full instruction in the duties and obligations of the state of life they are about to enter. The pastor is obliged to take special care to explain to them the duties of parents, the faithful fulfilment of which he urges upon them most earnestly.

Now the time has come; the bride has to approach the altar to give her hand to the bridegroom, that she may become his faithful companion for life. But the Church does not allow her to come near the sacred spot at once. After having in the preceding examination induced her to make a faithful preparation, and consequently to exercise herself in acts of devotion, she exhorts her now, on the eve of her wedding, to approach also the holy sacrament of penance and holy communion, in order that she may appear at the altar free from all sin and in perfect union with the Divine Saviour. And whilst taking the important step the Church is at her side. In her presence she has to enter the alliance, in order that it may become a sacrament and receive her blessing. It is by a sacrament that the Church introduces the bride into the state of matrimony, in order that by its mysterious influence this state may be sanctified and become the soil, as it were, from which children may spring up in holiness, and that through its beneficial working the parents, and above all mothers, may become enabled to educate in a truly Christian manner the children whom God will confide to them.

This is the way in which the Church acts

with regard to matrimony and the vocation of mothers. It is holy in her eyes. Hence her care and endeavor to cause it also to be regarded as holy by married people, and especially by mothers, to be regarded as a state to be entered holily and to be preserved holy.

Happy the virgin and the wife who make this preparation at the hand and according to the will of holy Church. When the time comes to fulfil the duties of her vocation as a mother, then she will prove to be a truly Christian mother, and great will be the blessings which she will spread all around. This was the school in which those mothers were trained whom the Church honors as saints —Saint Elizabeth, Saint Hedwig, Saint Monica, Saint Paula, and so many others.

But to prepare thus in the school of the Church for such an important state of life, for a vocation the effects of which reach into eternity, is, especially in our days, very much neglected, yes, even despised, by a great number. Where is the spirit of the fear of God and of piety to be found in many virgins? Alas, all their thoughts and desires tend toward dress, vain trifles, toys and pleasures! In how few is found fervor in prayer, fervor in visiting the house of God, in receiving the holy sacraments! How many are guilty of violating their most sacred duties towards parents; of spending time vainly and uselessly! And what is their innocence of heart? Alas, perhaps that jewel has long disappeared!

And what must be said of the time intervening between the betrothal and the marriage? Instead of using every means to prepare themselves as well as possible for such an important vocation, those who contemplate marriage too often pass that period in adding sin to sin. And how do they at last appear before the altar of God? Alas, the levity of the period preceding reaches even into the nuptial day. Not the least sign of that holy earnestness appears which would be becoming here. What is worst of all, do not many, in consequence of unworthy confessions and unworthy communions, receive the sacrament of matrimony sacrilegiously? It is horrible! To enter the state of matrimony with a threefold sacrilege, with a threefold mortal sin!

How can the blessing of God be expected? How, above all, can such brides be expected to become good mothers? Alas, experience teaches that the unfortunate children of such marriages have mothers who, instead of imbuing them with the spirit of the fear of God and of piety, rather become by word and example the cause of their ruin.

NECESSARY CONDITIONS.

THE Christian mother is, as we have seen, with regard to her children the minister of the Church. As it is the duty of the Church to lead the faithful in the path that leads to their salvation, so it is also the duty of the mother, in union with the father, to use all possible means to secure the salvation of her children. Man has a twofold destiny: he is destined for this life upon earth and for a life in eternity. He has a natural and a higher, a supernatural, destiny. To speak more correctly, however, there is but one destiny for him—the supernatural—to arrive at which the natural must serve as a means. Hence it is the duty of parents, and especially of mothers, to train their children from their earliest years to the attaining of this twofold destiny. The mother must therefore begin at once, as far as lies in her power, to give to the child a suitable education in all that is necessary or useful for its success in temporal matters, for its personal welfare, and for its success in human society; but far more is she obliged to instruct the child in the way it must go to arrive at its supernatural, eternal destiny, so that it may grow up a worthy member of the Church, and thus one day be admitted a member of the kingdom of heaven.

This, then, is the real, the highest duty of the mother, viz., together with the father, to train her children in the true fear of God and in the practice of solid piety. Whatever else might be regarded an object of care for a mother in respect to her children is, if compared with this, quite insignificant; for just as much as the life of eternity is longer and consequently of more importance than this short, passing life, in so much the education of the children for eternity—that is to say, their training in the fear of God and in piety —surpasses in importance their education in the pursuits of this life.

To educate her children from their tender

years in the fear of God and in solid piety is then, in fact, the highest duty, the true vocation, of a Christian mother, the most important point in Christian education. Should a mother have taken all possible care and succeeded in educating her children in the most desirable manner for this world; should she have enriched them with all desirable knowledge and skill, that they might move with ease in society, in perfect accordance with the requirements of their state and condition; if she neglected or was incapable of implanting in their hearts at the same time a fear of God and piety, we would be forced to say she has not fulfilled her duty; she has not done what was required by her vocation; she has not been a good mother to her children. How great one day will be her responsibility before the Sovereign Judge! And her children, however skilful and useful members of society they may be, in whatever high esteem they may be held by men, are nevertheless very much to be pitied; for whatever they may have received from their mother, the best, the most essential, the one only really good thing has been kept far from them.

The fear of God and piety ought then to be the precious dowry of a Christian mother to her children. To give them this is the most essential duty of a mother, and to fulfil this duty in a satisfactory manner she stands in need above all of two things, which we shall proceed at once to consider. The one is to be herself animated with the spirit of the fear of God and of piety; the other to be possessed of a true love for her children.

THE MOTHER'S FEAR OF GOD AND PIETY.

In order to communicate to her children a right and good education the mother must herself be possessed of the fear of God and piety; for how can I give what I have not myself? How will a mother inspire her children with the spirit of Christian piety if she herself be void of it? Or how can one give instruction to another in what he himself is ignorant? Let us take the most insignificant things as examples: a trade, an art, a science; to instruct others in them we must, as every one knows, first have been instructed in them ourselves. Is it different with regard to the fear of God and piety? It certainly is not. There is here, on the contrary, a far greater necessity than in all other things of being previously instructed before instructing others. He alone who has himself learned and acquired the fear of God and piety is capable of instructing others therein, and so important is this truth that it is necessary to look at it more closely.

To begin: will a mother who is herself wanting in the spirit of Christian piety take any care to awaken and foster this spirit in her children? No one will ever accomplish anything truly good unless he takes an interest in his work. Here is the reason why so many parents—or to speak of mothers only, why so many mothers—take little or no care of the godly fear and piety of their children. In many houses children learn how to keep house, the useful arts, and how to behave among educated people; but they learn nothing of what belongs to a truly Christian life; of what would render them pleasing in the sight of God. They are not taught the Christian virtue of zeal, urged by which they are careful to say their prayers in the morning and evening, before and after meals; the virtue of love and respect for the house of God and sacred service; they learn nothing of the exercises of a Catholic life. They hear scarcely anything of all this from their mothers. And the reason of this sad condition is the mother's indifference for these things.*

It is then clear that, in order to expect a mother to give her children a religious education, she herself must first be animated with a lively fear of God; for it is then, and then only, that she can be expected to take upon herself all the pain and trouble which is inseparable from the work of education, which to be a constant and faithful one will always require many and great labors and sacrifices. Not a day will pass without requiring many acts of self-denial,

---

* Not long ago I met a sprightly little boy; and while speaking to him, I learned that he was six years old. I asked him whether his mother had told him about God, heaven, and our Saviour. The boy knew nothing about them. Then I asked whether he knew the "Our Father," the "Hail Mary." He answered, "No." Whether he could make the sign of the cross. "No." "Poor boy," I thought to myself, "six years old and still ignorant of all this! What parents must his be! What kind of a mother must he have!" I insisted on him telling his mother that a priest begged her to teach him the "Our Father," the "Hail Mary." Afterwards, as I had asked his name, I called his priest's attention to him.

if a mother be in earnest about directing her children in useful occupations; about inducing them to frequent school and the Church; in teaching them the necessary prayers; in watching carefully over them; in keeping them far from bad companions; in instructing, admonishing, rebuking, and punishing them. The mother who is not well grounded in true piety will soon find all this too troublesome; she will prefer a comfortable, easy-going life, which she does not like to have interrupted by the care of children. Hence she will give them only that attention which is of strict necessity.

But as the religious training of children can be expected only of a Christian mother, so also it is only from her endeavors that success can be expected. A truly and sincerely pious mother is the one who is chiefly capable of speaking a language that can be understood by a child, and such as will go to its heart. The more her own heart is filled with the love of God and glowing with the desire that her dear child may also love and serve God, the more easy she will find it to descend to her child's inexperience and find expressions that can be understood by it, and the deeper will her words sink into its heart. How deeply, too, do the instructions and admonitions of a truly pious mother descend into the child's heart! They are like so many seeds of blessing for its whole future life.

But alas! how cold and unimpressive are the words of a mother whose heart is estranged from God! If after all she should still speak of Him and of religion to her children, her words will leave them unmoved.

A right and good education is, moreover, in itself a very difficult task. How could it be expected that all parents, all mothers, should be sufficiently acquainted with and capable of putting into practice the rules and maxims that must regulate the successful education of children? But if the mother be under the guidance of the true fear of God, then her heart, illuminated by faith and God's grace, may be relied upon, for the most part, to tell her at once how she has to proceed in the education of her children, and her pious life will be a school for the children in which they will receive more and better education than could be given to them by the inculcation of many rules and maxims. Hence the fact that a child who has truly pious parents will not easily degenerate in course of time, whilst, on the contrary, the degeneracy of children who have perhaps received a liberal and worldly education, but who have not enjoyed the benefit of good example, is often very great. To this must be added that the child, especially in its tender years, is much less, if at all, susceptible of religious instruction and admonition by word of mouth, and that it understands better the language of its mother's example, not to mention its great inclination to and facility in imitating whatever it notices in her. God Himself has planted this great imitative quality in the child's heart, in order that it may the better learn from its mother whatever is necessary, expecting that she will not exhibit to her child's eye anything but what is good. If, then, a mother be truly pious, her ordinary daily life will be a school for the child wherein it will learn the manner and practice of a Christian life even before it can understand them, so that when it arrives at an age to comprehend them it will perform them the surer, the more steadily following its mother's salutary example.

Thus from its tender infancy the child will learn from the mother, and through her pious example, to love God and our Saviour; to raise with respect and confidence its little hands to Heaven: to esteem and frequent the house of God and divine service, to be charitable and benevolent to the poor, to be industrious; to love labor, order, and cleanliness, those pillars of Christian piety; to cherish mildness, clemency, affability, truthfulness, and whatever other virtues may shine forth from her.

Happy, therefore, the child that has a truly pious mother; her life and example is for it a school wherein it becomes almost imperceptibly initiated and instructed in all the ways of a Christian life. And how deeply all that is learned in this school of example sinks into the child's nature, becoming an indestructible foundation on which a truly Christian life will rise like a lofty and solid edifice!

But the child that has not from its earliest years enjoyed the salutary influence of a good mother, and of her pious life, will scarcely ever become a good and fervent Christian. On the contrary, its mother's coldness and indifference with regard to God and virtue will be communicated to the child; and how then can the icy crust be broken that has formed around the young heart? How then can the child be inspired with interest for God's holy religion and for virtue—that is, for that of which it has heard or seen at home but little or nothing, and which has remained unknown to it in those years when the heart is formed and the will given a certain direction? Indeed, it is the greatest misfortune for a child to have a mother who does not care about God, nor about religion, nor a Christian life. Would to God that all Christian mothers understood how surpassingly great is the importance of being imbued with a sincere fear of God and with true piety themselves! How earnestly would they then be impelled towards them! Then also would they feel that as often as God confides children to their care, the call reaches them to become good and pious themselves; for only these children will become truly good and pious whose mothers are so, and their goodness and piety will be the greater as the goodness and piety possessed by their mothers increases. The greater progress a mother makes in true and solid piety, the better is she fitted to give to her children a good education, and to lead them to the higher degrees of perfection Are not the many Saints whom we have mentioned sufficient proof of this? They had holy mothers, and it was to them after God that they owed their sanctity.

Arise, then, Christian mothers, behold the sublimity of your vocation, the aim of which is nothing less than to lead those children that God has confided to you to heaven, to God, and fully aware that it is impossible to fulfil this duty except you yourselves are attached to God, your Lord, serve Him faithfully with your whole heart, sparing no trouble to make continually new progress in His love, in the accomplishment of His holy will, and in all Christian virtues. Let it be the object of your most earnest, fervent prayers that God may assist you more and more with His powerful grace.

LOVE OF THE MOTHER FOR HER CHILDREN.

It is idle for us to make any preliminary remarks concerning a mother's love. Where could a mother be found without love for her children? Love, the most tender, the most heartfelt, is but the natural companion of motherhood! Nothing short of the greatest degeneracy of a mother's heart destroys it. Its absence betrays something contrary to nature. But it is not this natural love that at present challenges our attention; it is the supernatural love of a Christian mother for her child that we are to speak of, in so far as the possession of this kind of love is a necessary condition for a mother. To fulfil maternal duties requires more than a mere natural love; a higher, a Christian, a supernatural love must exist.

The mere natural love of a mother for her child is not only insufficient, but, in as far as it is not transformed into the higher and Christian love, it too often becomes an impediment to the discharge of her duties, and sometimes the very cause that they are not fulfilled at all or in an unbecoming manner. Nor would it be difficult to find instances where her natural love has prevented the mother from doing what the true welfare of the child demanded. How often does it not happen that a mother, though she loves her child with this natural love almost to excess, neglects to do what alone would make it truly happy and educates it in a manner that leads to destruction! Must not this be said of all those mothers who seek only the temporal welfare of their children and spend all their time and labor in securing for them temporal advantages? Again, must not this be said of all those mothers who, in order to procure for their children temporal goods—for instance, an office, lucrative employment, and the like,—even go so far as to expose them to the imminent danger of falling into grievous sin and of losing their innocence and faith?

From an imprudent, unreasonable love for their children, many mothers cannot bring themselves to punish them, as they should to keep them in due subjection, or to refuse them anything, however much reason and prudence may require that their unruly desires be checked. Often they permit them to follow their own will, even in what may be hurtful to them; and they nourish in them, through this imprudent complacency, improper habits and defects. If when meeting persons that are victims of sin and misfortune we could read on their foreheads the first cause of their misery, how often would we not make the sad discovery that this misery must be traced back to the blind, irrational love of their mothers!

Indeed, this natural love of mothers for their children, if not overruled and sanctified by grace, has been and continues to be the cause of the temporal and eternal ruin of innumerable children.

From this we see how true it is that as the tender love of a mother for her children is a necessary condition for the fulfilment of her duties, since it imparts courage, patience, perseverance, and zeal in all those difficulties, labors, and sacrifices connected with her vocation, so also is it necessary that this love, in order to become truly productive of good, be invested with a supernatural character—that is to say, that it be a Christian and supernatural love. This latter love proceeds from faith and grace. All those properties which are found in a mother's natural love are also found in her supernatural love, but ennobled, as it were, glorified, and in a higher degree. If we graft a twig of an improved variety on a fruit-tree, the twig will develop in proportion to the vigor of the trunk; the tree will become finer, and the fruit more delicious. Such a vigorous trunk is the natural love of a mother; ennobled through faith and grace, and changed into supernatural love, it will produce all the fruit of the natural love, but in a nobler, a higher degree; for the truly Christian mother, when looking at her child with the eye of faith, sees in it also a child of God. As by its natural birth it has become *her* child, so by its supernatural birth in holy baptism it has become also a *child of God*. Yes, it is far more the child of God than her own. Hence all the love which a Christian mother cherishes in her heart for God tends also by virtue of God's grace towards His child, and since the mother loves it also as her own child, it follows that that higher and supernatural love unites itself with her natural love, elevating and glorifying it.

This is not all. The Christian mother recognizes in her child also a little brother, a little sister of Jesus Christ, the God-Man; she recognizes in it the darling of His Sacred Heart. She knows how much Jesus, the great Friend of children, loves little ones, and among them her own child, and how dear it is to Him. The more, therefore, she loves her Saviour, the more she will love, because of Him and in Him, her child with an elevated and ennobled mother's love. Her faith assures her that her child is a member of the great community of Saints; that therefore all the Saints in heaven, Mary the Queen of heaven above all, and with her all the elect, interest themselves in her child; that they love it as their little brother or their little sister, and that they burn with desire for its salvation. She knows also that those sublime, celestial spirits, the holy angels, unite with the love of the elect for her child; that one of their number is even destined to be its special friend and guardian. Will this not, must this not, make the darling of her heart unspeakably more dear to her?

Her faith makes her behold in the child

the image of God which was imprinted upon its soul in holy baptism, when it was born anew by God's sanctifying grace. She beholds in it one who has been redeemed by the blood of God's only Son. She beholds in it a temple of the Holy Ghost, and beholds Him mysteriously reigning therein by sanctifying grace. She looks upon her child as an heir of heaven, destined to partake for eternity in the joys and delignts of the house of our common Father. Must not all this make the child of her heart precious to her beyond measure? Must it not make the child appear in her eyes as something truly great and sacred? It cannot be otherwise, and ever afterwards her eye will rest with a certain reverence upon her darling. Her mother's heart will thrill with holy joy, and with the help of God's grace its love will become wonderfully elevated, and at the same time glorified. With the fervor and ardor of this ennobled, sanctified, and supernaturally elevated love she will fold the child in her arms and press it to her heart.

This is then, according to God's holy will. the love which a Christian mother must have for her child, and it is the one which alone corresponds to her vocation. God is always ready to give His special graces in order that the mother's natural love may become transformed into such a supernatural love. This transformation is one of the effects of that grace which is given in the holy sacrament of matrimony, and if a mother continues to renew and increase divine grace in herself by faithfully giving her time to prayer by frequently assisting at holy mass, by approaching often and worthily the holy sacraments of penance and communion, or by other exercises of piety, it is then above all that her *mother's love* will be renewed and increased. The soil in which the love of a Christian mother takes root is divine grace, to this it owes its existence, its growth, and its supernatural character. Those very truths of faith which lead a mother to love her child with a supernatural love, and nourish and increase this love, receive in the end their true light and efficacy through grace.

We see now what the true love of a mother, the supernatural love of a mother, is. It is the work of God in the mother's heart. He who has planted in her heart a natural love has also by His grace and truth changed this natural into a supernatural love, and at the same time glorified and increased it; and if the work of nature, the natural love of a mother, because of its great efficacy excites our admiration and veneration, how much more magnificent, beautiful, and great are its effects and fruits!

"Love is strong as death." This word of the Holy Ghost is verified by the natural love of a mother for her child; but how much more by her supernatural love! Just as a mother is animated by a truly Christian spirit will the love which she has for her children be invested with a supernatural character; the more true is it that no pain for her child, no labor, no difficulty, no trouble or sacrifice, will be too great or too difficult for her. However great the burden may be which the child imposes on her, however great the privations which it requires of her, and however much it may rob her of rest day and night, she will never lose her cheerful courage; she will persevere willingly and indefatigably; she will never give way to impatience and anger; she will endure everything; she will submit to everything; she will be ready to sacrifice even life itself for her child. How truly do the words of the apostle in regard to Christian love in general apply to the Christian love of a mother! "Charity is not provoked to anger, is patient, beareth all things, endureth all things, is kind, seeketh not her own."

The mother sympathizes with her child's affliction, and allows herself no rest until she has conquered it. She rejoices in the joy and happiness of her child. This is true in general, but more especially, and in a far deeper sense, with regard to the welfare of her child's soul.

The truly Christian mother beholds in her child, as we have already seen, also the child of God, confided to her by the great Father in heaven. It is her vocation to lead it back to Him; as far as lies in her power she must make every effort that the child may arrive one day where He dwells Himself. It is the supernatural love for her child that causes her to do this. In virtue of this love the highest object of her care and industry is to rear her child a perfect child of God, to keep it far from the greatest of evils, from sin and eternal damnation, and to lead it towards obtaining the highest happiness, the glory and bliss of heaven.

There is nothing that a Christian mother desires more earnestly than that her child may remain free from sin, and that, should it unfortunately have committed some faults meriting God's displeasure, it may free itself from them at once. She watches also most carefully the beginnings of bad habits, not allowing them to take root in her child. It was thus that Blanche, the pious mother of St. Louis, the holy king of France, thought and acted. When the child was given back to her after baptism, she pressed it to her breast and said, "My child, you are now a dwelling of the Holy Ghost; would to God that this dwelling may never become profaned through sin!" When Louis grew up she endeavored to inspire him with a great hatred of sin, and used to repeat, "My son, I would prefer to see you robbed of the throne—yes, even of life—rather than know that your heart was soiled with one sin." We know the effect of this holy mother's love: the son became a Saint.

There is no suffering, no pain, no evil—

this is the conviction of a Christian mother—that can begin to be compared with the sorrow, the pain, the evil, which sin and moral corruption bring to the child. Hence nothing is so far from the true love of a mother as imprudent tenderness and forbearance whenever there is question of preventing or of casting out sin. The Christian mother consequently does not hesitate to keep her child in strict discipline, to refuse it many things, to punish it, yes, even to subject it to bodily chastisement, as often as she thinks this to be the only means of preserving it from sin or to advance it in virtue, since the love she has for her child is a ray of that love which God has for men, and the love of God for us never prevents Him from punishing us if necessity requires. On the contrary, "those whom God loveth He punisheth," as Holy Scripture says, and " He chastiseth every son whom He receiveth." It is the same enlightened love that enables the Christian mother to watch over her child and guard it, as much as lies in her power, from whatever could expose it to the danger of suffering injury in its soul at home or abroad, through frivolous discourses, bad examples, dangerous companions, suspicious amusements, or from any other cause.

That the child may grow up in true piety and in the fear of God is the highest, greatest desire of every Christian mother's heart, when ruled by a supernatural love. The greater and the more sincere this love is, the greater will also be the mother's endeavor both by word and example to accustom the child from its earliest years to the practice of all good, to impart a continually increasing acquaintance with the truths of our holy religion, and to increase within it the love of God, true charity, and every kind of virtue. For as the mother, through her natural love, is much concerned in the temporal welfare of her child, so she is still far more concerned for its soul, and that it may prosper and persevere in a life pleasing to God, knowing full well that without the fear of God and without genuine piety solid happiness cannot be secured even in this world.

If love thus calls forth the most zealous and most earnest endeavors of a mother for her child's welfare, it also keeps up and increases in her the zeal of prayer in behalf of the child; for whatever such a Christian mother does for her child, she will never say, "It is enough;" she will always try to do still more; she desires for her child a still greater happiness than that which she can herself procure for it. It is for this reason that the love of a mother never ceases to appear again and again before the throne of God, to obtain for herself and for her child whatever she regards desirable for its happiness.

Enough has been said to show of what high importance in the vocation of a mother is true and enlightened Christian love. Its presence is the condition necessary for the fulfilment of all the duties of her vocation, and enables her to perform them in a more perfect manner and with greater success. Of it may also be said what the Holy Ghost says of wisdom: "With her all good things are come together to me." And the more a mother's love is endowed with the supernatural character, the more fruitful will it become in those wholesome effects just mentioned.

Is there not to be found in this a powerful inducement for every mother to nourish and to increase her supernatural love for her children? This she does by every exercise of a Christian life. If the love of which we are speaking can be found to exist only in a truly Christian mother, it will also receive a proportionate increase and perfection by every advance in Christian piety. But it will also be directly increased and preserved by the consideration of the truths of our holy faith to which we have before made reference. They should therefore be very often made the object of reflection and consideration by Christian mothers. Mothers' should make it a practice to look often at their children with the eye of faith. Whatever this glance discovers in them is highly proper to endear them still more to their hearts. But especially should the Christian mother often entreat the Lord to elevate and to change by His grace more and more her natural love, and to enrich her with a most perfect and ardent supernatural love for her child. But we shall return to this subject.

THE MOTHER'S DOWRY FOR HER CHILD.

WHEN a son or daughter, having arrived at a mature age, is about to leave the parental home, to enter the state of matrimony, the provident love of parents furnishes them with all things necessary for establishing a new and separate household. This is called the "dowry." It is not, however, of this dowry that we intend speaking here, since at present we are considering the tender child only and a mother's influence on it. There is a dowry of a different kind which is furnished by parents, and especially by the mother, to the very babe. When after baptism the child is brought home, the mother receives it into her arms with a heart full of gratitude. Henceforward she beholds in her child also the child of God. By virtue of this regeneration the child has become endowed with sanctifying grace, the most precious treasure of heaven, and with all those privileges and rights which are contained in it. This is the dowry of its heavenly Father and of its spiritual mother, the Church, now and forever.

But from its parents in the natural order

the child has also received a dowry when entering this world, consisting of their own natural qualities, perhaps even peculiarities. They pass in a mysterious manner from the parents to the child. Look at this child. Is it not the image of its mother? The same countenance, the same eyes, the same forehead, the same features; and when grown up, what a great similarity in size, in formation of the body, in gait, in behavior! It is as if the mother had become young again in the child. In a similar manner, but far more strikingly, the child inherits the spiritual qualities of the parents, and above all those of the heart. Let a mother be of a quiet, mild, condescending, benevolent, and merciful disposition; let her be a lover of order and cleanliness; let her be of a tender conscience, and be truthful and just,—and you will easily discover in her children, if you observe them closely, from their earliest youth the same dispositions and qualities. If the mother be penetrated by sentiments of sincere fear of God and piety, then the child may be expected to enter this world with a certain natural disposition for Christian piety. This is what we mean by the *dowry of a Christian mother* for her child; it is certainly a most precious dowry.

But what we have said with regard to a mother's good qualities must also be said of her evil ones. They too descend to her children. If you trace back the origin of the many bad habits and evil inclinations so often sorrowfully discovered in the very bloom of childhood, you will frequently find that the first and real cause of all these is in the mother,—and perhaps also in the father. The mother is stubborn, self-willed, irritable; the child also. The mother is vain, a lover of finery; the child is likewise. The mother is given to lying, is greedy after enjoyment; the child too. The mother has opened her heart to the spirit of uncleanness, and alas! the child too gives early signs of a similar inclination. The mother is dishonest, faithless, fraudulent, she stretches out her hand after her neighbor's goods; the child becomes a victim to the same vices. Thus it seems as if the mother had planted the germs of her own vices in the tender heart of her child. Her faults bud forth already in the tender child; an inclination to her own vices is something belonging to its very nature.

Here we behold a dowry of another kind, but alas! an unenviable one for a mother to leave her child.

This fact cannot be denied. Proofs of it are found in every family. No doubt these natural, inborn faults and virtues are not of themselves real faults and virtues. The child is not yet pleasing to God on account of the latter, nor displeasing on account of the former. But how greatly do not these help and assist the child to acquire one day true Christian virtues and to make great progress in them, or to fall the easier and become the deeper immersed in vice!

It is true, no one who has become a slave to vice and sin will ever find before God an excuse in the vehemence of the natural inclinations which he may have inherited from his parents, since God is always ready, when his innate, inherited bad inclinations make it more difficult for him to avoid sin, to give him also a greater abundance of graces in order to gain the victory, requiring only of him that he should use faithfully the means at his disposal to obtain His special help. Every one with God's assistance can work out his salvation. But alas! does not sad experience show that those who have innate bad inclinations permit themselves too often to be carried away and be overcome by them? Experience shows also that innate good inclinations are a great help in the exercise of virtue, and to enable a soul to arrive at a high degree of perfection.

What a great reproach for a mother it is to see, as it were, imprinted in her child her own bad habits, faults, and sins! How great must not be the bitterness of her heart, should she, as it too often happens, be compelled also with time to suffer many harsh and disagreeable things from the bad habits of her children, and be forced to confess, "I am myself the cause of my present sufferings from my children! I have prepared this rod of correction myself"! And how great must not be her grief and sorrow when those bad inclinations which her children inherited from her have developed into strong passions, and threaten to cast them not only into temporal but also into eternal misery!

Herein is contained an earnest admonition and a duty for the Christian mother—and also for the Christian father—carefully to avoid everything that may be wrong and wicked, to free themselves more and more from their faults in order to save their children from so sad a dowry ; herein is contained the most powerful motive to be diligent in the exercise of virtue, and for the acquirement of whatever is good, in order that a natural disposition to virtue may be the dowry for her child.

This heritage of the faults and virtues of the mother is in fact not to be ascribed exclusively and solely to the influence which the mother by word and example exercises over the child, but also to that mysterious disposition, established by our Creator, in consequence of which the mother communicates to her child her very being, just as she communicates to it the natural life which she gives to her suckling babe. Yes, whilst this communication of what belongs to her body takes place, the mother communicates to the child in a mysterious manner all the dispositions of her heart, the quality of her soul in a general manner, and in particular that quality which prevails at the time preceding its birth. And thus it happens that the mother, even before the child is born, exercises that wonderful influence on its heart and character which is so often made unquestionable by experience, viz., that the sentiments, the dispositions of heart, which were those of the mother at the time preceding the child's birth often appear in the child in a most striking manner.*

How important, therefore, is the duty of a Christian mother to keep holy the weeks and months before the child's birth! How carefully they should avoid every inordinate emotion and sinful action! How anxiously should they attend to the exercise of Christian piety! How great should be their fervor in prayer, in assisting at Mass and other divine services, in receiving the holy sacraments, and in the practice of all kinds of good works, especially in works of mercy!

---

* There are instances of children remarkable for their great inclination to steal, whose mothers during the time preceding their birth were guilty of theft. A certain young man had a great liking for spiritual things, and was pious in a very remarkable degree, whilst all his relatives without exception were notably indifferent to God and religion. This young man afterwards entered a religious order. The discovery was made later that just before his birth his mother was very much impressed with the idea that she would soon die, and consequently prepared herself earnestly for death, which really occurred. Thus the mystery was solved.

Such, as we read, were the lives of the mothers of the Saints. Their mothers offered them to the Lord even before birth, following thus the pious inclination of their hearts, and accompanying at the same time this their offering with good works, and with fervent prayers in behalf of their offspring. And thus it happened that they brought forth together with their children, and in them, a certain inclination to sanctity, a treasure of the most precious kind. Some day it will become known how much this precious dowry, prepared by an excellent mother, has contributed to the sanctity of her children, and how great a share in their virtues and perfection and great deeds those holy mothers have. This will be for all eternity their glory and happiness.

Who does not see how great and sacred are those duties of a Christian mother which we have pointed out—duties the faithful and conscientious fulfilment of which is so essential in determining a happy or unhappy lot in time and eternity? And the reason we have determined to treat of this matter, notwithstanding a certain aversion which we feel toward it, is because it touches essentially the cause of the true welfare or the misery of children! Would to God that our effort be not in vain! May it contribute towards inducing Christian mothers to become more and more anxious to lead truly Christian lives, to banish out of their hearts and conduct every sin and sinful inclination, to give themselves up to the practice of all kinds of virtues, and thus become enabled to procure for their children that dowry which consists in the natural disposition and inclination of their heart toward virtue.*

---

* To prevent all misunderstanding we subjoin the following note: If we lay so much stress on what has been said about those natural inclinations and dispositions for virtues and vices which children inherit from their parents, we are far from giving any credit to that impious theory of materialists, who wish to know nothing about God or an immortal soul and grace, and who therefore regard virtues and vices as nothing more than manifestations of dispositions which are deeply rooted in our physical nature. The real origin of virtues and vices is to be found, as has been already indicated, in the immortal soul and in its relation to divine grace. But notwithstanding this, the natural disposition of a man and even his body—which disposition perhaps many a time has been inherited from the parents—has often a great influence on the soul as well in the exercise of good as in that of evil, so that, in consequence of the natural, inherited disposi

THE CONSECRATION OF A MOTHER.

IF we desire a plant or flower to grow, it is necessary that the surrounding atmosphere be of a quality corresponding to its peculiar nature. Thus it is that the most beautiful flowers generally thrive only in a

tions for good or evil, the good or evil deed may commonly be expected or feared sooner and easier in some cases than in others. Who does not see of how great importance, therefore, these inherited dispositions are, although it is ultimately the free will of man, which, if it corresponds to God's grace, performs good ; if it resists God's grace, performs bad actions. And as a man, though he be gifted with the best natural dispositions, if he be not assisted by God's grace, cannot do anything truly good, so if assisted by God's grace he will be able to overcome the most obnoxious and the most perverse inclinations. It is for this reason that no one will find an excuse for his sins before the judgment-seat of God in the power and vehemence of his natural inclinations. God is always ready to assist men so that they may overcome their bad inclinations ; they need but to entreat Him in a becoming manner for His help. It is ultimately man's own fault if he falls into sin and loses his soul. But if it cannot be denied that certain bad inclinations have been the proximate cause of sin and perdition for a child, will it not be a bitter reproach for a mother if she is compelled to say, " These strong and bad inclinations the child has had and still has through me !"

mild southern climate. And in the spring would not everything die and wither away were the cold north wind continually to sweep over the fields and dampness and cold prevail, and were the rays of the sun to remain powerless? So also in a home a corresponding atmosphere must prevail if what is good in the child is to come forth and develop. In addition to the supernatural life, Almighty God has engrafted in the tender heart of the child in baptism the germs of the heaven-born plants of faith, of hope, and of charity, and the virtues contained in them. There they must grow more and more, and bring forth blossoms and fruits worthy of eternal life. The house of the parents is the enclosure to which these heavenly plants in the child's heart are almost exclusively confided during its childhood. Here they are hidden, and thus it may easily be seen that everything requires a proper atmosphere to exist in it; in other words, that here a truly Christian spirit should reign, that in all the relations and conditions of the family life the ruling of truly Catholic sentiment should make itself felt. And that this should really be the case, especially in the first years of the child—in those years properly called childhood—depends almost exclusively upon the mother.

It is God's merciful will that a Christian atmosphere, so to speak, should pervade every Christian household, in order that these precious germs of Christian virtue may unfold and grow, blossom and bring forth good fruit, and that the child's heart may thus become truly consecrated in a Christian manner.

Let us imagine a child who from its most tender years has been in such a truly Christian family, who has lived in a home where everything was full of the spirit of a Catholic fear of God and of true piety, so that it never saw nor heard anything contrary to this spirit, but was rather met everywhere, in behavior, in conversation, in the doings and omissions of the other members of the household, even in the furnishing of the house, with the influence of a truly Catholic spirit, of a truly Catholic taste and sincere piety; would it not be almost impossible for a child living under such influences to grow up with a different spirit and to lead a different kind of life? Such an effect has the atmosphere of a truly Christian home beyond doubt; it is of immense advantage to the happy and truly Christian development of the child; it gives to the tender heart of the child in truth a certain kind of consecration, the consecration of a Christian heart.

Rise, then, Christian mothers! create as much as it is in your power a Christian atmosphere within your homes! This belongs particularly to you, since the child is, as we have indicated before, in its earlier decisive years *especially*, yes, often *exclusively*, given to your care. The behavior of the mother, her conversation, her manner of acting, her example, her management of the family, these create the atmosphere for the little ones. Happy for her and for her children if she understands how to make this atmosphere truly Christian and Catholic, that is to say, truly wholesome for her children. And this is accomplished by every truly Christian mother.

The very house has, through her endeavors, a Christian outfit. Therein we meet, at least in the principal rooms, religious pictures, a crucifix, perhaps a statue of the blessed Virgin Mary the Mother of God, and of some Saints. There one sees a vessel for holy water, probably also blessed candles and the like. The child notices all these things, becomes inquisitive about them, puts questions, learns from its mother the signification of them, receives from what it sees and hears salutary religious impressions, and becomes thus quite early and imperceptibly accustomed to a Catholic life—a consecration of the young, tender heart.

But far more does the true, genuine, practical Catholic *life* of the mother create this wholesome atmosphere for the child. It observes that the mother prays, that she goes to church, to instructions, to confession, and to holy communion. It sees how, before and after meals, the mother devoutly folds her hands and prays; and all this very soon becomes sacred in its eyes, for the very reason that it is done by its mother, and it feels itself impelled to do the same; it tries to imitate its mother as closely as possible. Or the child notices how industrious the mother is; how carefully she preserves order and cleanliness; how, when exposed to difficulties and troubles and sufferings, she maintains her peace of heart and bears everything patiently, so that it never hears from her lips an impatient, angry expression, far less anything like profanity. It sees how its mother conducts herself with great compassion, mildness, and affability towards all the persons of her household; how much goodness she shows towards strangers; that she is always ready to oblige and please them, and how willingly she assists the poor. All these things are so many silent exhortations for the child, which delights in always doing as its mother does, and thus, without perhaps a single word of direction from her, it is induced and encouraged to begin to practice all those virtues that shine forth in her, and thus the germs of these virtues, which God has laid in its heart, begin to thrive and grow.

And the same may be said of all other actions of the mother with regard to her child. In fine, whatever a truly Christian mother does is for the child a salutary, wholesome influence, which causes the germs which God has planted in its heart to shoot up and grow continually, whereby from its earlier years a reverent esteem and love for religion is instilled into it. This, then, is the *Christian consecration of the child's heart*. The influence which the uninterrupted Christian conduct of a mother exercises on her child descends deeply into its whole nature. This influence engenders in its heart effects almost imperishable, so that in many respects it is to be valued much higher than exhortations and other influences. Happy the child that has experienced this in itself! A happiness, a grace, wherewith nothing upon earth can be compared.

THE CHILD'S INTRODUCTION INTO THE TRUTHS OF OUR HOLY RELIGION.

WHEN the child, still under the shelter of the parental roof, is, as it were, breathed upon from all sides by a Christian spirit, it will unconsciously live according to this same spirit; its heart will, almost imperceptibly, receive a Christian constitution.

But the mother conducts the child into a Christian life by the use of direct means also: by teaching it the truths of our holy religion.

Conscious that the first efforts and noblest part of the child's being belong to God, and that God has confided the child to her, to educate it for Him, the mother endeavors to incline its heart and mind early towards Him and heavenly things by teaching and instruction.*

* Not long ago we read a letter wherein a good, pious, Christian virgin, to whose care the little children of a noble family are confided, expresses herself with regard to the smallest of her wards as follows: "The little child is becoming so interesting; it can already fold its little hands so prettily when I say morning prayers with it, and it listens with a very earnest look to every word I say, and begins to repeat some of them." We do not wish to conceal that these words have quite moved us. Would to God that every mother acted in the same manner toward her children by beginning in their tender years to lead them to God! We cannot deny ourselves the consolation of giving an extract from a letter of a young mother, a former pupil, to whom we had sent a copy of this book: " . . . I felt great pleasure in reading the little book. I found and have already begun to put in practice many of the counsels given to mothers. Permit me to mention some instances: Our little Mary, who is now one year and eight months old, knows already how to bless herself alone, and can say the short prayer, 'Good God, make me pious, that I may go to heaven.' She prays also for mamma and papa, grandmamma, grandpapa, and uncle. And when I ask her, 'Little Mary, where is God?' she answers, 'There, above, in heaven; if little Mary's good, God will bring her up to heaven.' Whenever she sees a crucifix, she desires

It is indeed wonderful how great the susceptibility of children is for things relating to God. Even when still too young to have a right and perfect understanding of the truths of our holy religion, there is, as it were, in the inmost part of their being a chord that vibrates when one speaks about God, of our dear Saviour, of heaven and heavenly things. They listen with a pious avidity, and the impression made in their hearts becomes depicted upon their faces. It may be said that God Himself has tuned

to kiss the good God. We rejoice over it. My husband, too, who is a civil officer, assists me faithfully; for instance, when he brings the children to bed he makes them first fold their little hands and pray. He does the same before and after meals. . . . To my good mother, too, I owe much for having urged me from childhood to all that is good. Even now I say every morning, with a few additions, the same 'good intention' which she taught me when I was a child. . . . How often do I not feel myself impelled to pray to God that he may preserve little Mary in her innocence! When I look at the little innocent creature slumbering in the cradle, I often weep, and I shudder when thinking of the danger to which she may one day be exposed. Then I feel forced to entreat God that He may help me and my husband to educate the little one so as to become a good and faithful Christian. In this also the dear little book will help me. I shall make diligent use of it."

the strings which vibrate on such occasions in the child's heart.

This is the reason why the notion is false that children in their tender age ought not to be troubled with such things as surpass their understanding. It is true they do not yet understand them as grown persons do, but they understand much more than is usually supposed; they understand enough about them for their age; they hear and learn them with advantage. Thus it is that the heart is won to God and lofty aspirations in those early years which shape its whole future life. In time they will also come to a perfect understanding of these truths. On the other hand, how difficult it is to implant a true love for God and heavenly things in those who have reached mature age without hearing the divine truths! It may be that they will learn and understand them, but their hearts will remain cold.

The little child soon begins to grow; it learns to speak; it can walk alone. The mother willingly follows this development of the child's natural life with instructions and directions corresponding to its spiritual wants. She tells the child much about God and our divine Saviour.*

Thus when the mother is sitting in her room, or by the fire, or in summer before the house, bending over her work, with her little child playing or working near her, or perhaps standing before her, resting its little arms upon her knees, watch how it keeps both eyes and mouth fixed on her, as she speaks to it of those dear things; or on Sunday, whilst the rest of the family have gone to church, the mother sits down with her little one to spend her time with it in pious conversation, or in a leisure hour she takes it by the hand and they go into the open fields; then she calls its attention to all those beautiful things that meet the eye, and tells

* How our Lord is God as well as man, and that out of love for men He himself has become man and a little child; how He was born; how as an infant and as a young man he acted towards His mother and St. Joseph; how He assisted them in their labors; how at all times, even when preaching His divine doctrine and working miracles, He loved children so much; how He called them to Him, to embrace, to caress, and to bless them, and the many beautiful things He said of them and to them; and how He at last died for us all on the cross, but rose again from the dead and is now in heaven, desiring very much that we too should one day come there and be happy with Him for all eternity.

how the good God and Father has made them all, and how beautiful He has made everything, here plants and flowers and fruits, there little birds and animals, and how, in fact, He has made the whole world.

If the mother herself has a liking for these things, she will not find it difficult to speak about them. Her simple language, easily understood by the child, will sink more deeply into its heart than the formal instruction received in school; especially when the mother knows how to accommodate herself to her child's manner of thinking.

As yet little accustomed to thinking, the child receives what is intended for its comprehension in the easiest and best manner by means of its senses. The judicious mother therefore uses such impressions to lead her child to the knowledge of higher truths and of the doctrines of our holy religion. She shows it pictures which represent what she is about to relate. She explains these pictures and what is contained in them, and the child thus comprehends it easily. For the same reason she from time to time takes the child, when yet young and tender, to church, especially before and after solemnities. Although the child understands but little of what it sees and hears, it receives a salutary impression, especially if the mother tells it that the church is a sacred place, that our divine Saviour dwells therein, that we must behave in it very devoutly, either bending the knees or standing with hands folded. Before leaving she will show her child many things: pictures, paintings, statues, altars, pulpit and confessionals, at Christmas the manger, at Easter the sepulchre. And on reaching home she will explain what the child has seen in church; this with the answers to the questions which the child asks about what it has seen will offer occasion and matter for the most salutary instruction.

What opportunities and helps a mother has for giving information to her child, especially by the feasts and solemn times of the ecclesiastical year! How can a mother regard it a difficult task, on the days preceding the feast or on the feast-day itself, to explain to the child, at least in general, what is its signification and meaning? If she does so, the child will by degrees, during the time of our Lord's Nativity, in

Holy Week, on Easter, on the feast of the Ascension of our Lord, on Pentecost, become acquainted in a vivid manner with the history of our Saviour and with the mysteries of His whole life. On the feast-days of the blessed Virgin it will learn more and more of the Mother of our Lord and how to venerate her. And how much matter for very useful narrations is offered in the lives of those Saints whose names are daily mentioned in the calendar, especially if the mother be inclined toward reading them!

Besides this, a mother who has a love for God and religion, and who knows the duty of leading her children from their earliest youth to God, will never want occasions to speak in this manner. And how can she excuse herself with a want of time for such occupation with her little ones, or with not knowing how to go on? Is a mother required to occupy herself with her child in the manner spoken of for a great length of time? The great utility of such communications does not depend upon their taking place very often and at a sacrifice of much time; the "too often" and "too long" become even positively injurious; but it may be found in this, that the child hears those things which are so necessary for it from the lips of its mother when still young, and thus at the same time becomes acquainted with them and learns to live according to them, and upon the fact that the mother speaks of these things on occasions like those we have just mentioned. And no mother will want time for this; nothing but a good will is required.

But she does not know how to do it! What is there to be known? Cannot the mother tell her child at least what she herself knows? And should that be ever so little, it will produce innumerable blessings. And why should not the mother, if she knows but very little, endeavor for the benefit of her children to learn more by reading, or by listening to sermons and instructions? Is not this in the end her duty?

The real benefit does not so much depend upon the lesser or greater amount of religious knowledge that the mother can impart to the child, but rather on this, that the child hears her speak of God and of higher things at the very dawn of consciousness and after this period also—that is to say, long before it is ready to attend school—and that its tender little heart in its first affections is drawn toward them; that it hears of them from the mother or father, and not from any one else, so that the innate reverence and love for its parents becomes also transferred to what it hears from their lips, things which cannot be too highly appreciated.

Much is that child to be pitied that in its tender and decisive years, those years which precede the period at which children are usually sent to school, hears and sees at home almost nothing relating to God and heavenly things. If its heart while yet tender has remained cold and closed against God and higher things, will it at a later date open to them? If it has never heard anything of God from its parents, whose behavior was its only rule and model during its tender years, will it not like its father and mother remain perfectly indifferent to all this? Oh, what an irreparable loss! what an immeasurable misfortune!

If what we have indicated shall be put into practice, it is necessary beyond all doubt that the mother herself must also be animated with a sincere fear of God and with piety. This is an essential condition to the right and true development of the child; without it such development will be totally impossible. But a truly Christian mother will reduce our instructions to practice almost spontaneously; she will do it the better, and consequently with greater success, the more she is animated with a truly Christian spirit.

We are forced to repeat therefore, constantly, that almost everything depends upon the possession by our mothers of a true and genuine Christian fear of God, and of piety. Would to God that all mothers knew this, and consequently made all possible endeavors to obtain that without which they must become unfaithful in the performance of their most sacred obligations to their own and their children's perdition.

HOW TO BEHAVE WITH REGARD TO THE FAULTS OF CHILDREN.

WE have more than once called attention to the change in the child's heart when, by the grace of God and through the merits of His redemption, it is born again through the regenerating waters of baptism. It is changed, as it were, into a blossoming garden, wherein our Lord has planted precious seeds of Christian virtues, plucked from the soil of His own Being, which shall grow into a greater similitude to Himself. This truly divine creation is confided by the Lord to the parents, and during the first years especially to the mother, in order that they may care for and cultivate it.

But alas! together with those heavenly germs are also found the germs of weeds, the sad inheritance of our first parents, perhaps also of the very parents of the child. "And when the good seed grew up the weeds were also seen." We refer to the evil inclinations of human nature, inclinations which were corrupted by our first parents' sin, and which, according to the adorable counsel of God, are not taken away by baptism, but must be conquered by man himself with the aid of that grace which is promised to every one in holy baptism, for the greater increase of his eternal happiness. And the power and strength of these evil inclinations, in so far as they have their origin in the sin of our first parents, become easily increased and augmented in consequence of the high degree to which they may have been developed in the heart of the father and the mother by the sins they themselves have committed and through the irregularities in which they lived at the time the child was born to them.

These weeds already begin to show themselves in the tender child in all kinds of irregularities and faults. Who can possibly be ignorant of this? Can it escape the attention, above all, of the mother, if she be not blinded by an irregular love for her children? It is therefore her duty, and the most essential part of her vocation, to be attentive to and to resist at once the child's bad inclinations with all energy, resolution, and prudence, and with an indefatigable love. If this be not promptly done, evil inclinations will become stronger and the child's faults more grievous, and its heart will become the fertile soil of all kinds of sins, whilst the germs of virtues, implanted in that same heart, will miserably decay. Would to God that all mothers were sufficiently aware how important, how necessary, it is to begin at once, at the very time of their children's tender childhood, to treat in this manner their faults, and to induce them in the right manner to rid themselves of them! If, when the child does wrong, there were questions about some isolated or occasional faults only, there would then perhaps be less to be feared; but in the case of the tender child there is question about faults that are rooted deeply in its heart, about faults which have their origin in bad inclinations which, once permitted to manifest themselves, will soon become very powerful and will beget a kind of habitual, fatal necessity to commit such faults again, and which will plunge the child finally into great sins and crimes.

At no other time does a fault take deeper root in man's nature than in his early childhood; no fault is more difficult to be conquered and extirpated than that to which one has become accustomed as a child. Who does not know the adage, "As is the child, so is the man"? If a child in its first years be permitted to be wilful, disobedient, jealous, selfish, spiteful, malicious, cruel to animals, dainty, a glutton, vain, disposed to lie, all these faults will become strong with time and in a manner a part of its nature, so that there is little hope that they ever will be conquered. On the contrary, we have to expect rather that they will increase with the child's growth, springing up ever anew like poisonous weeds, preventing thus the growth of a truly Christian being.

And yet with how little difficulty could not all these weeds have been rooted up in the tender years of childhood! This, then, is a very urgent duty for a mother and her special work, since she has more opportunity and, after all, can do this more skilfully for her child in its tender years.

She must, therefore, have an eye on the faults of her little ones. If any fault becomes apparent in them, no time must be lost in merely looking on and waiting. The mother must never think, " The child is still young ; it understands nothing about it ; later on I will correct it." Oh no! The sooner reproof begins the better; one will succeed in it by beginning early. There is no need that the child should understand the grievousness of a fault ; it is sufficient for it to know that it is not allowed, that the mother, the father forbids it, and thus it gradually forgets it and becomes free of it and remains out of its reach. The mother then should never allow her children to go unpunished for their faults, even though they have not yet come to the use of reason. Let her tell the little ones with all the love and tenderness of a mother, "You are not allowed to do that; that is not right;" or, "That is not pleasing to God; if you do it, you will not be a good child;" or, "If you do that, it will not go well with you; you will not be happy; you will not go to heaven," and the like. Should this not have effect, then she must speak more seriously; she must threaten with punishment. Should this, too, be of no avail, the punishment must be inflicted in all earnest, more or less severe, once or repeatedly, and continued just as success may require. A truly Christian mother regards it as a sacred duty to rid her children as soon as possible of their faults, and does not hesitate to have recourse, if necessary, to punishments, even to severe ones, and to bodily chastisements. Should her natural feelings, her feelings as a mother, rebel against such means, she knows, nevertheless, that she is not allowed to be guided by them; that it is

God's will and her own duty to despise them whenever the true welfare of her children may require this of her. This is true, enlightened, Christian motherly love: to punish a child in order to rid it of its faults.

No doubt the love of a true mother will lead her as much as possible to employ mild means for the correction of her children; but, should these means not succeed, then she will not hesitate to adopt more severe ones, and even corporal punishments. Is it not in fact cruelty to a child if a mother from false pity, fearing to cause the child a passing pain, allows it to go on in its faults, becoming thus herself the cause of her child growing up with them; with such faults, moreover, as will mar its happiness and prepare for it great misfortune? Who has a greater love for men than God? And after all, how severely He punishes them from time to time! "Those whom I love I chastise."

The more deep-seated the fault appears to be, the more rigorous must often be the means employed, and with the greatest perseverance. Of what avail is it if a mother admonishes a child of its faults, and even punishes it from time to time, and then ceases to care about it; or if she punishes it once or twice, but much oftener lets the faults go on unnoticed and unpunished? Perseverance in punishing a child's faults is no doubt very often accompanied with great self-denial and great sacrifices. It is generally much easier to let a child go on with its faults. But let the mother remember that without trouble and sacrifice a truly Christian life cannot be imagined, and that in so important a question as that which regards the child's welfare it is doubly her sacred duty to submit to them and to persevere until success shall be secured.

It is true that many mothers cannot be said to be indifferent to the faults of their children. They oppose them, but in what manner? Almost always, especially when the children become guilty of some more grievous faults, they permit themselves to be carried away with indignation and anger. A current of angry words and expressions is let loose upon their children, without a suitable prudent punishment; or if a punishment is inflicted, it is in a fit of anger, so that it easily becomes excessive and even cruel. How sad such a proceeding is! It is self-evident that such action can never bring the child to rid itself of its faults in a satisfactory manner. On the contrary, it will be productive of great damage. For what will become of its respect for its mother if it sees her always angry and a victim of blind passion? How can the tender love of the child for its mother continue if she rushes upon it so cruelly? And yet respect and love are necessary conditions for a successful education! Bad examples, coming from a source where a perfectly good example is a sacred duty, increases these evil effects.

Would to God that all mothers considered earnestly how strictly they above all others are bound to master anger in the presence of their children! Should this, however, owing to circumstances, be very difficult, as for example, when the mother is of a choleric temperament, then our Lord will also be ready to give her special help, so that she may be able to persevere in mildness and patience. Therefore, Christian mothers, often renew your good intentions! Never desist from imploring God's help.

A good mother patiently bears with all the faults of her children, and however great may be her endeavor to eradicate them, she is always calm and cautious; she never forgets that they are children, and that they will commit faults, and that for this reason their guilt is not so great. But she will never allow herself through such forbearance to be induced to abstain from a severe mode of proceeding against them. She always acts quietly, with presence of mind and discretion, against these faults, now advising, now warning, now punishing, but never with passion. And the more she corrects and chastises her children in a peaceable manner, the surer will she suceeed. The children will more and more understand that their mother is acting only from detestation of their faults; and they themselves will learn to abominate their misdeeds, so that not only the fear of punishment but also this aversion of their faults will keep them from committing them again, and their amendment will become thus surer, and love for their mother will also remain undiminished.*

---

* We may here mention some of the faults of children. *Stubbornness* takes the first place. It delights to insinuate itself into the hearts of children, and it must be attacked at once with all possible energy by every good mother.

Certain faults prevail in the child with an obstinacy which seems to defy all the pains and trouble taken by the mother. Ought

She accustoms her child to be obedient to its father's will. What once has been said or ordered—after mature reflection—that is firmly adhered to, *that* the child *must* do, let come what may, should it even be necessary to use very severe punishment. Woe to the parents if a child becomes aware that it can succeed by insisting on its own will! Wilfulness, that great evil and impediment to all that is good, will grow out of it. The danger of giving way through unreasonable love to hurtful indulgence is mostly greater on the part of the mother than on that of the father. Therefore, Christian mother, be on your guard! When there is need to break the stubbornness of a child, then it is your sacred duty to despise natural feeling. Be assured your child will thank you one day for it. To be early accustomed to obedience is the condition and guaranty of obedience to God, that is to say, of a Christian and consequently also a happy life.

After stubbornness comes *vanity* and *love* for *extravagant dress*. How pernicious and injurious does not this fault appear to be in grown persons! Not to mention the loss of time and money which cannot be separated from it, it exercises also a very bad influence on the heart, and becomes the cause of its affection for vain trifles, toys, and unmeaning ornaments, of its losing more and more the taste for God and higher things, and is, alas! too often the cause of one easily losing the precious treasure of innocence, and becoming a victim to moral wanderings. And how often is not the cause of these misfortunes laid in childhood, by the child's very mother! She has allowed the child to go on with its inborn vanity; she has even nourished and promoted it. And is it not rich nourish-

she to lose courage, give up her endeavors, and let things go on just as they may? Most assuredly not! What does not a ment for vanity when the child notices how often and with what great interest the mother speaks of dress and finery; what importance she attaches to them; how much trouble she takes to obtain them, and what great gratification she finds in them; or if it sees that the mother makes much ado about its own dress, spending on it so much care, money, and time, and this with as much importance as if there were question about its soul's salvation?

No one that is prudent can doubt that it is the duty and vocation of a mother to accustom her children to order and cleanliness as regards their dress, even to give them a taste, so to say, for a certain nicety in their dress, and even for grace and beauty, since this may have a wholesome influence on the moral nature, whilst want of order and of cleanliness becomes too easily a help to immorality. But not less binding is the duty to avoid whatever could directly increase vanity and love for finery in children. The mother acts, therefore, wrongly and injuriously to the child if she makes too much ado about its dress; if she spends unreasonably much time and money on it; if she admires the child too much in its new dress, especially if she intentionally dresses the child in a remarkable manner, so that it may be distinguished from other children; for in all this she excites the child to vanity, and is even guilty of vanity herself. Can we, therefore, be surprised at seeing the children of such a mother running full speed into the disorders of vanity? He who has to live in a great city too often meets with children fixed up by their foolish mothers in such a fantastic style that one is tempted to take them for the children of comedians.

mother do when her child suffers from bodily infirmities? She leaves nothing untried to free it from them; she uses all

What kind of spirit is nourished by fancy dresses of this kind? Certainly not a Christian spirit. And how little regard is there not often paid to tender and Christian modesty and purity! O Christian mothers, do not act so cruelly with your children! Do not so deliberately nourish vanity in them to their ruin! Observe a certain modesty and moderation in the manner of dressing your children, not neglecting the requirements of your state of life! Accustom your children early to know that the true and most beautiful ornament of a person consists in the possession of a pure, sinless heart, enriched with Christian virtues. Woe to you if you yourselves practise vanity along with your children, by adorning them immoderately in order to make them outshine others! Is it not imperilling the true welfare of your children in order to satisfy your own vanity? Is it not causing damage to your children's souls in order that you may flatter the vanity of your own hearts? Indeed, you are something like those heathen mothers, who throw their children—sacrificing them—into the red-hot arms of Moloch.

Let us pass to another fault which is too often found in children, the *habit of telling lies*. Is it necessary to set forth the hideousness of this fault? Love of truth and hatred of falsehood belong essentially to the true Christian spirit. No one who is in earnest with his Christian profession will ever go so far as to lie. He who cares little or nothing about truth shows clearly that he is very far from perfection. Do you think it possible that the blessed Virgin Mary would ever have descended so low as to tell the least falsehood? She would have preferred to sacrifice her life. To this must be added that telling lies is the road to many

possible means, and resorts to every physician who she thinks can aid her. And is she to remain unconcerned in diseases which are far other sins. Well, then, Christian mothers, oppose these faults in your children; let not one of the misfortunes springing from these faults come upon them. Children easily give way to lying, and if they are not opposed they will soon get into the ignominious *habit* of it. Therefore caution your children; show them at a proper time the hideousness of falsehood; insist firmly on their saying always and in all things the strict truth. Whenever a lie escapes their lips, do not neglect to reprehend and punish them. Induce them to confess their faults whenever they have told a lie; if they acknowledge sincerely and with regret the fault committed, then mitigation of the punishment, perhaps even full pardon of the fault, should be granted. Be it far from you to give your children an example in yourselves of telling falsehoods, or even of inducing and directing them in this shameful practice! May God's blessing enter every house where falsehood is hated and proscribed!

Perhaps one or the other of your children suffers from an irritable and passionate disposition, is easily carried away with anger, becomes excited, uses insulting language, curses, rages, and the like. If not opposed in this propensity to anger, which is one of the capital sins—that is to say, one of those faults which usually is the soil in which many other sins of a grievous character are produced—it will become stronger in it. How difficult it will be to conquer when it becomes, as it were, the child's second nature, and how much will it not interfere with the happiness of parents and others! Should you, therefore, Christian mother, become aware that your child is suffering from this fault, do not be slow

worse—the diseases of the soul? Oh no! She cannot but hope to see her children cured of them. Should her endeavors alone not be to check it and to drive it out at once. Admonish, instruct, blame, reprove, punish—over and over again—according to the greatness of the fault. Do not cease until by God's grace you have succeeded. To be sure, should you yourself suffer from this fault; should your child, being itself inclined to anger, see perhaps too often how you are giving way to angry expressions, or perhaps even experience the effect of your passion, under such circumstances it cannot be expected that your reproofs will avail anything. Alas! you push your child only deeeper into its faults, you confirm it in them. Woe to you!

With the fault just alluded to another may be said to be connected, viz., a certain *uncharitable, selfish behavior*. This shows itself in the child's conduct toward brothers and sisters. It is selfish; it cannot bear to see anything good happen to its sisters and brothers; it delights in taking what belongs to them; it is unkind, disobliging; it hurts their feelings by word and deed; and it cannot live in peace with them. Or this ill-nature makes itself felt toward other children, or toward all with whom it comes in contact. It has no compassion for its neighbor's sufferings; it cannot bring itself to give anything or to assist other children when it could do so; it easily quarrels and disputes with them, calls them names, insults them, causes discord among them, and fights with them. All these faults are the fruit of that selfishness and want of charity which belong to corrupt human nature. If suffered to remain, if not opposed, then that egotism, which in our time tyrannizes over so many, will become implanted in the child, and it will remain deprived of that virtue which belongs to the firm constitution of a Christian

sufficient, then she looks to the father for assistance; she consults with prudent and experienced persons, and begs for their assistance. And should all this not be crowned with success, she may yet have recourse to the Lord, who is a powerful helper. In Him, as at all times, especially now, she takes refuge; she entreats Him with unceasing prayers to hasten to her help with His mighty grace to break the child's bad spirit and free it of its faults. "For all things are possible with God," says our Lord.

life, viz., true charity for our neighbor. How much cause there is to lament its absence on earth! And yet without true love for one another no one is a true Christian, nor has he any hope of being saved. The cause of this sad condition is too often found already in the child. It has been left by its mother to go unpunished for its faults against charity, and has not been accustomed to the practice of it towards its neighbor.

Christian mothers, regard it as the most important point of education to bring your children by instruction, exhortation, warning, reprehension, punishment, and prayer to avoid and rid themselves of all that is contrary to charity, in the first place with regard to brothers and sisters and other members of the family, and in the second place with regard to all men. Let them look at you as examples of true, heartfelt charity for one another.

THE GUARDIAN OF HOLY MODESTY AND INNOCENCE.

LOVERS of rare flowers, when in the possession of a great number, keep if possible a hot-house. Therein, especially during the colder seasons of the year, are kept plants belonging to a warmer climate, in order that they may be sheltered from the inclemency of the weather, and that its balmy atmosphere may render them thrifty.

Such a hot-house should every Christian home be rendered by the care of the mother —for the protection, for the shelter, for the growth of one of the most precious, most beautiful, most sweet-scented of flowers. This flower, descended from the far-off country of heaven, Jesus, our Lord, brought down upon this earth and planted in the flower-garden of His Holy Church. There it has bloomed from the beginning, in order to gladden by its rich fragrance the heart of God, as also thousands of human hearts. It is, alas! of a tender nature; it suffers too easily from the cold breath of this world and its wicked influence, so that its beauty fades and its fragrance disappears, and at last it becomes miserably blighted and dies. It is for this reason that for it, too, as it were, a place of shelter or hot-house is required. The Christian home ought to be such a nursery or shelter, and the Christian mother its protector.

What is this precious flower of heaven? It is holy purity, the virtue of chastity. Who does not know and value its dignity? Who is not attracted by its beauty? Who does not rejoice at the fragrance which it spreads around? For it is this virtue that creates the most perfect peace in those hearts that are consecrated by its presence; it is also the firm and solid foundation of true happiness in life, the surety for the love of God and his grace, the surest guaranty for obtaining salvation. Where is there a virtue that spreads around itself so many blessings as that of chastity? But it is a very tender virtue, most like a tender flower which is injured by the lightest touch and by the least breath of cold. Therefore it is that according to the will of God the Christian home must serve as its sheltering-place and protection; there it ought to be carefully guarded; there, especially by the vigilance of the mother, everything ought to be refused entrance that could injure it; there it must be fostered and cherished. And for this reason this chapter is entitled, *The Guardian of Holy Modesty and Innocence.*

Alas! in the world, especially now, there is no provision made for this heaven-born plant. It is menaced by a thousand dangers. A thousand persecutions are prepared for it. There storms rage, there coldness domineers, there the brood of all kinds of sinful vermin crawl about. There holy innocence, the virtue of chastity, is most easily lost. Woe to it if even in the bosom of the family protection should not be found for it! if in the sanctuary of the Christian home dangers are also lying in wait for it! No, the Christian father, and still more the Christian mother, is anxiously careful that at home a holy discipline be found always and everywhere, in words and in actions.

Here a holy discipline reigns in conversation. No double meaning, no indecent word is permitted. Unbecoming jokes are unknown. Unbecoming things and occurrences are never spoken of.

Indecent conversation, jokes, and songs are in themselves blamable and sinful, and, as the Apostle says, should not be even named among Christians, still less be talked of. But to say nothing of the damage, how great is the ruin which such conversation and jokes cause, both in those who utter them and in those who listen! They are a very pestilence; they are seeds of lasciviousness sown by frivolous tongues in the hearts of men, to shoot up into immodest thoughts, desires, and words. There is no doubt that the cause of perdition was laid by immodest conversations and jokes in the souls of thousands that are now wallowing in the mire of vice. Drive out of this world immodest jokes and conversations, and thousands, who otherwise would groan in the service of vice, would never lose the precious treasure of chastity, but by its blessings would be happy for time and eternity. "Evil communications," says the Holy Ghost, "corrupt good manners." What a judgment without mercy will, therefore, await those who are directly or indirectly guilty of such conversations by not preventing them when they could!

Immodest conversations, jokes, and songs are never suffered in a Christian family, but are shunned and guarded against most carefully. The mother regards it as her sacred duty to exercise in this regard an anxious watchfulness, and to insist with all earnestness and rigorous strictness that no immodest word shall ever be heard in her family. She has a watchful eye on the servants and laborers, in order that they may not hold, which is, alas! too often the case, immodest conversations in the presence of her children. Should such a thing ever happen, it ought not pass without an earnest and severe reproof, and the servant or laborer disregarding this ought to be dismissed as soon as possible. How many children and how many of the younger servants through the levity, frivolousness, or wickedness of such men lose their most precious treasure!*

* At the funeral of the wife of a farmer living on the boundaries of Westphalia, the pastor related the following about the deceased: A new servant had been admitted to the farm. Although when engaging servants great care was usually taken to admit only such as were supposed to be possessed of the fear of God and piety, nevertheless they had been deceived on this occasion. The new servant had an unbridled tongue, which very often gave utterance to lewd expressions, and as the custom of such

Woe to the house where such conversations are held without opposition in the very presence of the mother; or, still worse, where parents are themselves frivolous or wicked enough to join in them!

It is also one of the rules of a Christian house that scandals of a certain nature which may have happened in the neighborhood or community are not to be mentioned, and above all not in the presence of the children and of the younger members of the household. Ah, why is greater caution not used in speaking? Children are, alas! very curious; they listen with great attention to indecent conversation; they strive to catch every word; they think about what

creatures is to indulge in their wicked practice on every occasion, even at table, he gave proof of his foul heart. The lady of the house made it clearly understood that such things were not suffered in her house, still less in the presence of her children. But to no avail. The filthy, dirty expressions were repeated. The lady went quietly behind the chair on which the wicked servant was sitting and boxed his ears well. That had its effect. If this was rather uncivil, we should remember that our divine Saviour also scourged certain people, and we believe He would do the same now, were He on earth, to many of those of whom we have spoken. At all events, it is our duty to proceed in earnest against such a disorder.

they hear; they inquire about it and speak of it to their playmates; and thus an unguarded expression which they have heard at home will be too often for them the cause of great sins. "Behold," says the Apostle, "how small a fire kindleth a great wood."

The Christian mother insists also on modesty and decency in dress. There is no question about fashion; immodest dresses are never permitted by a conscientious mother. We speak here only of that bad habit, which is met with in many houses, of appearing before others, for instance in the morning after rising, or in summer when the weather is hot, or at certain occupations, without being sufficiently covered. By this decency and good morals are undoubtedly violated. Mothers ought to insist that their children never leave the bedroom without at least being dressed in such a manner that decency and modesty may not suffer; that they may not have good reason to blush when seen by strangers. How much it is to be deplored to see children in the morning almost half naked, and even outside the house! If this is dangerous for their health, it is far more so for the tenderness of their sense of modesty, which is of so great importance, but which under such treatment will by and by disappear. So also, in summer, comfort or convenience can never be a sufficient reason for a mother to allow her children to take off their clothes in a manner that may be prejudicial to decency.*

The importance of preserving untarnished holy purity, the virtue of chastity and innocence being so great, a holy discipline must therefore be preserved on all sides. This discipline requires that all familiar and consequently dangerous friendships of the two sexes be carefully prevented, The Christian mother will as much as possible avoid letting children of different sexes sleep alone in the same room. Sleeping together in

---

* It is very desirable that ladies should appear in the morning as they wish to be dressed during the day. Should this not be possible, then they should at least appear dressed so as not to be ashamed of being seen by people out of the house. Nor can greater comfort or ease give any right or title to appear before others in a dress that could be considered as not according to the requirements of holy modesty. These are hints which undoubtedly merit to be considered in many houses; hints the contempt and disregard of which are followed by many sad falls.

one bed, always suspicious even with regard to small children, is entirely unjustifiable after children have arrived at the age of discretion. God alone knows how numerous and great misfortunes must be ascribed to this. How is it possible that many parents act so inconsiderately in this matter, as if they had neither reason nor conscience! Not less wrong nor less worthy of condemnation is it for parents to allow their children, after they have grown up, to sleep with them in the same room. Every one who considers, however superficially, to what great dangers the innocence of children may be exposed by this negligence, how easily they may suffer the shipwreck of their sense of virtue forever; how much, at all events, their sense of modesty will be injured, must come to the conclusion that it is the sacred and strict duty of parents to do all that is possible and to spare no trouble to procure for their children separate sleeping apartments. This is indeed a matter of the greatest importance, important enough to be proclaimed from the housetop.*

* Conscientious masters will also take care that their male and female servants have their bedrooms at a proper

Those who may consider what has been said as exaggerated and inopportune are certainly not aware of the ruin which the neglect of these precautions has caused in many souls. Not to understand nor to care about these things is at least a dangerous thoughtlessness and too often a criminal indiscretion, and indicates a great want of conscientious feeling.

But, besides, how little respect and care is paid to modesty in many homes; how many things are done and permitted by which it gradually becomes tarnished! We would not venture to speak of this were we not certain that the importance of the matter gives us a right to do so. It is then, for instance, wrong for a mother to allow indecent uncovering of her children when they are sitting, lying down, or playing. The children may have no evil thought when doing so, but the sense of modesty will always suffer by it. What great want of shame is often seen among grown-up persons, among even

distance, and that there be no occasion for keeping dangerous company. In fine, it is the duty of masters to use all possible care to prevent all that might be dangerous to the virtue of their servants.

fathers and mothers, in regard to such matters! It is simply unintelligible; it shows how much the sense of modesty has become blunted in them. But in truth, this sense of modesty has been planted by God in man's heart that it may be fostered and become strong, and be, as it were, a barrier against the floods of impurity, a wall of defence for innocence against all that could endanger and injure it. If this wall has been pulled down, this barrier been swept away; if this sense of shame has disappeared from man's heart, then it will stand open to the spirit of uncleanness and to all those vices that accompany it; then the heart will be ripe for every sin, and, if occasion offers, will certainly fall. It is therefore of the greatest importance that this sense of holy shame be preserved intact in children; that it be fostered with all possible care; that it be kept tender, and that everything be avoided in the house that might endanger it.

Would to God that what has been said might be everywhere received and attended to with due regard, so that holy modesty, innocence, and chastity would find in Christian families a place of refuge and in the case of the mother a kindly protection! The more the spirit of impurity reigns and threatens to destroy all holy living and all real happiness on earth, the more should holy discipline reign in our homes! Then, with God's help, it will be verified that in such a house a chaste generation dwelleth; chaste, honest parents, innocent children, and modest servants; and of such families what the Holy Ghost has said will also be verified:

"Oh, how beautiful is the chaste generation with glory! for the memory thereof is immortal, because it is known both with God and with men. When it is present they imitate it, and they desire it when it has withdrawn itself; and it triumpheth, crowned forever, winning the reward of undefiled conflicts." (Wisd. iv. 1, 2.)

THE MOTHER'S DIRECTION OF HER CHILDREN.

LET us suppose that a gardener has by chance come into the possession of some rare seeds. These he has planted in his garden; they germinate; the tender shoots come forth from the earth. Will he from that time remain unconcerned about them? Certainly not; on the contrary, he will continue to exercise great care over them; every day he will look after them frequently. Not satisfied with anxiously keeping from them whatever might be hurtful and dangerous, he does what he can to insure their growth and to make them develop into the perfect beauty and splendor of their species. An excellent suggestion for Christian mothers and fathers! But what are the most beautiful flowers when compared with those tender plants which God Himself has planted in the child's heart? They are, as it were, seeds from the garden of heaven, germs which God in His infinite goodness has taken from His own majestic, adorable Being and laid in man's heart in order that, developing therein more and more into the majesty of Christian virtues, they may change man into an ever-increasing likeness to God. The mother is called to be the gardener. It is on this account, therefore, that the mother, as we have seen, is most anxiously concerned in freeing the child's heart from the weeds which threaten to injure or to hinder the life and growth of these heavenly germs of virtue.

But she does still more. As the gardener does not stop after having freed the beds on which his precious flowers are growing of all noxious weeds, nor after having sheltered them from all injurious influences, but continues to foster and cherish his pets with all possible care, not omitting anything that may promote their growth and development into greater beauty, in like manner also the Christian mother makes it her chief concern, as it is also her sacred duty, to do everything in order that the Christian virtues in the hearts of her children may become stronger and develop into greater perfection. Although the Lord has planted the germs of these virtues deeply in the child's heart, it is necessary that, as soon as the child comes to the use of reason, it should coöperate with God's grace and labor itself at the development and perfection of these virtues. It is here that the mother must give her child instruction and an early impulse. Without this instruction and impulse the good seed laid by God in the child's heart will scarcely develop, and certainly not arrive at perfection. It will be like a precious seed which does not grow, like a plant without life, withering away.

Enemies of our holy religion have tried to prove that faith, piety, the love of God, conscientiousness, chastity, and other Christian virtues are but mere habits derived from parents or others, from the fact that without impulse or direction from without these virtues do not exist. Oh, foolish men! Though the care and trouble of the gardener, the wholesome influence of the soil and of the air, and rain and sunshine contribute to bring about the development of the germ and the delightful flower, the soil, the rain and sunshine are not the cause of this effect; all these things together would never have brought forth the flower if the germ had not been first buried in the soil. In a similar manner also are the Christian virtues planted by God in the child's tender heart; but besides this, a number of wholesome influences from without, especially from the parents, and particularly from the mother, are needed in order that they may grow and flourish as they ought.

Here is another and a beautiful task for

the mother! She is called to assist the child as much as lies in her power, in order that the virtues which our Lord has planted in its heart may be active from the first dawn of its reason; or, what is the same thing, she is called to instruct her child that, as soon as it arrives at the use of reason, it may in all its doings at once and always show itself a Christian and prove itself to be a child of God by living a Christian life in harmony with the doctrines of our holy religion, and may at once begin to believe and hope in God and love Him. She is also called to induce her child from its earliest infancy to love all men; to show good-will, mildness, compassion, and pity to all; to behave modestly and humbly; to practise Christian patience; to learn to master and conquer itself; to become accustomed to spend its time usefully; to be always truthful, faithful, and sincere; to respect the property of others; to be just, righteous, honest, and to acquire all other qualities that belong to and adorn the true Christian.

And should the mother while her child is young live unconcerned about all this? Should she permit her children to live as they like for a number of years, perhaps until they have arrived at mature age, without troubling herself about inducing them to live as becomes Christians? There cannot be anything more absurd than this. Would you then leave for a time the grosser part of the child's nature, which is already inclined to evil and full of bad inclinations, to grow up and become strong, and allow what is higher and nobler in the child, the grace of being a child of God and the germs of Christian virtues, to remain uncared for? The natural and in many respects the wicked man, the heathen, you wish to prosper and grow, and the supernatural man, the child of God, the Christian, you propose to let remain little, undeveloped, a petty creature!

Do you not fear lest the Christian man, when at last it becomes necessary to think of caring for him, cultivating him, and inducing him to practise the Christian virtues, will be and will remain forever at the saddest disadvantage with regard to the natural, corrupt man who in the mean time will have grown up and become strong? "And Ismael persecuted Isaac" (Gal. iv. 29). And is it not the will of God that man should sacrifice to Him and to His service his whole life; that His child—for such man has become in holy baptism—from its earliest years, as soon as consciousness awakens in it, should prove itself a Christian and live like one and think, reflect, speak, and act in a Christian manner? The Lord loveth the firstlings, just these tender signs of Christian piety in a child;— how precious they are in his sight! Oh, what a misconception of things and truths, to have no care that the child may from its earliest youth prove itself worthy of its surpassing prerogative of being a child of God, of being a Christian! Let us look at the children of the powerful and great ones of this world. How great is the care that their children, as soon as they have arrived at the use of reason, should behave in all things in accordance with the rules of etiquette, of good morals, and with the special requirements of the grade of society in which they are expected to move. And should Christian mothers have no care that their children, who are children of the Lord of heaven and earth, behave even in their tender years in a manner that becomes the mode of life which reigns in God's kingdom, and according to the rules of Christian belief?

The first years of childhood, especially those immediately following the time when the child's consciousness has become awakened, are of very great importance, and are very decisive for the whole life. And should the child pass these years without being taught to live as becomes a Christian? How much is it to be feared, and how often does it happen, that those who have not lived as Christians in their childhood never attain to the happiness of leading a life which is entirely pervaded and ruled by a Christian spirit!

It is scarcely necessary to say that, whilst we even advocate the cultivation of a Christian life in tender children, we do not at all expect that this Christian life should manifest itself in the same degree as in grown persons. That would be requiring nothing less than an impossibility. But just because children cannot serve God and lead a Christian life according to the manner of grown persons, the mother must be a mediator for the child and point out to it how even in its tender years it can be a good Christian and practise the virtues of a Christian life. What has been said of the natural nourishment which the mother prepares for her child may also apply here. As God has ordained that certain kinds of nourishment which nature offers and which of themselves are not yet fit to be taken by the child are previously prepared by the mother, so in like manner ought the mother to bring the duties and practices of a Christian life to the child's heart in a manner corresponding to its tender age, and instruct it in them. This is a task for the mother which requires attention and a sincere endeavor, but which does not in any wise appear too difficult. To be sure, a mother who has not yet herself begun in earnest to lead a truly Christian life will never be able to fulfil this duty. It was just for this reason that we pointed out true Christian piety as one of the most necessary requirements for a good education. For a truly Christian mother, therefore, the task is not too difficult. To appreciate this let us as examples propose a few modes of fulfilling it.

Faith. The mother early instructs her child in the doctrines of holy religion, as we have shown, in a manner adapted to its capacity. This soon awakens the child's faith, and helps to develop it. Then she accustoms it to form its judgments about the value or vanity of things, and to govern its words and actions according to what it has thus learned of God and religion.

Suppose that the child has to suffer from temporal evils; the mother says. "My child, far worse than all these evils which you now have to suffer is sin." The child experiences some earthly pleasures and joys: "The joy of a good conscience, the joy of having done good, my child," says the mother, "is still greater." Or when occasion offers, she reminds it that God is with it, that He beholds it, that He is holy and just, etc.; she extols the great work of the divine love, and so on. Here your have so many exercises of faith. Besides this, she induces the child to pray that God may strengthen its faith.

Hope. The mother delights in relating to the child how many good, great, and beautiful things our Lord Jesus Christ has prepared and left in His Church for all those that belong to Him; when it grows up it will partake of them all, and thus become always better and more pious and more pleasing to God; then the mother will take it with her to Mass, where so many of these good things are to be found; in due time it will also learn many and beautiful lessons about our Saviour; when older it will itself be allowed to receive our Lord in Holy Communion. If it becomes very pious, God and our divine Saviour will love it very much. What happiness! And he will give it many good and beautiful gifts. Then the beloved mother of our Lord, the Queen of heaven, and with her all the dear angels and saints, will love it, and if it calls upon them, they will ask of God for it whatever is good and beautiful; and what happiness at last, when death comes! Then the beloved Saviour will haste to meet its soul, that it may enjoy with Him in heaven all possible joy and happiness. "If you pray now devoutly, and show yourselves very obedient and good children, then Almighty God will love you, and we may hope that you will enter one day into heaven." Or, if the child commits a fault—tells a lie or is disobedient—"Oh, my dear child, don't do that, I pray, or what will Almighty God, our beloved Saviour, think of you?

Children who tell lies, who are disobedient . . . where will they go one day? Certainly not to heaven!"

Charity. How many things are there in daily life that give joy and pleasure to a child; the mother reminds it pleasantly and repeatedly that all good things come from God, that it must give thanks to Him for them. The child knows of some who have done good to their neighbor; the mother, profiting by the occasion, says, "Oh, my child, how many more good things does not God give to me and to you!" Then she speaks of the goodness of God, of His mercy, of His being our Father; and of Jesus, how out of love for us he became man, suffered so much, even offered up his life, and continues still out of love for us to live, and work in the most blessed Sacrament. " Oh, my child you will never be able to love Him in return as He merits to be loved by you." Something perhaps may have given pleasure to the child; it values it very highly; it desires it so much because it is so beautiful. Again the mother, seizing the opportunity, says, "Oh, my child, how much more beautiful is God and our divine Saviour! He merits to be loved more than all creatures; what happiness, what joy to see and to possess Him one day!" Then she adds some instance of a Saint, especially of one, who died young, who loved God very much. At last she makes the child take the resolution to love Him always more and more,

Charity for one's neighbor. Above all should the mother induce her child to practise charity. In the first place, she must require of it to exercise charity towards all those who live in the same house; she insists with all earnestness and perseverance that it should avoid everything which might hurt the feelings of its sisters, brothers, servants, or any one living in the house; she suffers in it no sign of unkindness, of anger, quarrelsomeness, contention, revenge, or stubbornness; it must behave towards all with kindness and sweetness; it must exhibit a hearty compassion towards all who suffer, and be willing to divide cheerfully what it may have to dispose of with the needy. The mother insists also on a like behavior away from home; she never tires of reminding her child of it, and does not pardon if it neglects her advice. Inopportune reproofs of others, as they are never heard by the child at home, are not suffered to pass its lips. It is never permitted to quarrel and fight. It is required by its mother to be peaceable; it is taught to have compassion and mercy upon the suffering and poor; the mother gives it occasion to help them and distribute alms among them; she instructs it and leads it to be saving, so as to be able of itself to help and to give to others. The mother's example infuses this same life and activity in all.

What a great blessing for a child if Christian charity for one another thus grows up with it; if its selfishness and self-interest are crushed thus early in life! Why is almost everything at present governed by selfishness, charity and sympathy having disappeared? Because, while yet children, men were not made acquainted with nor taught how to exercise true charity.

From these few examples may be seen how a Christian mother may lead her child to practise Christian virtues. The same course may be pursued with regard to other points of a Christian education. The mother insists on the child being always and punctually obedient; on its telling always the full and entire truth; on keeping its promises; on being very modest, reserved, discreet; she induces it to bear with patience and resignation its little sufferings and trials; to be a lover of cleanliness, order, and occupation. "Our good God," she will say, "wishes children to play, but not always; they must also work, be diligent, and accustom themselves to occupation;* then, my dear child, go at once to your work."

With time the school-teachers come to the assistance of the mother in her work of education. What is more natural than that the

---

* It cannot sufficiently be deplored that this is so often almost entirely overlooked, especially by parents belonging to the higher classes of society. They permit their children to spend almost all their time in playing and running after amusements, and they show scarcely any mark of instruction or of care respecting occupation or labor. And what is the consequence? In after-life they fear labor, not being accustomed to it; and the bad consequences of this dislike of labor and of earnest occupation make themselves felt in a very serious manner in school, in their studies, in the household, and in their occupations. It need not be said that the kind and measure of work must be in accordance with the age of the children, and that a good deal of time should be allowed them for playing: but, notwithstanding, they must learn early to spend some time in working, in order that they may accustom themselves to work as one of their duties.

mother should regard and treat them as friends of her family and inspire her children with reverence and esteem for them, without which it is impossible that they should have a salutary influence over them; that she should never speak to her children of them with disrespect; that she should try to excite in the child an interest for what it does and learns in school, by examining it herself in what it should have learned, at the same time showing interest in its lessons.

The Christian mother teaches also the child to say its prayers as soon as it can, and instructs it therein in a manner corresponding to its capabilities. In like manner as did the lady whom we have mentioned, she teaches the child to fold its little hands and repeats some little prayer that it may thus learn it by heart. How beautiful and consoling if with the names of father and mother the name of God and the sweet names of Jesus and Mary are the first that pass the infant's lips! At any rate, children should learn how to make the sign of the cross and to be taught the "Our Father," the "Hail Mary," and similar short prayers, especially a short morning and evening prayer.* Once knowing them, they ought to say them every morning and evening.

The mother finds a pleasure in taking her child along with her from time to time to church, in order that it may learn to like the house of God and divine service, and to become interested in whatever regards them. The child should learn as much as possible the names and signification of the feasts, and thus become instructed to celebrate them, in order that it may be impelled to do so according to its yet weak capacity. The time has come when the child is obliged to go to church. The mother continually reminds it of its duty, and always insists on it going at the right time; she urges it to behave properly in church, and to say its prayers piously and devoutly. It is told to prepare itself for making its first communion. The mother takes the greatest interest in this; she in-

---

* Many mothers make their children say their morning and evening prayers in their presence. This is undoubtedly a beautiful practice. I remember with gratitude and pleasure how salutary an impression this pious practice used to make in my young and tender heart, when every evening our good mother brought us children into the bedroom and made us there in her presence say our evening prayers.

structs the child how to make its confession; she exhorts it to prepare itself well, and assists it in doing so. And whenever matters of greater importance for the religious life of the child present themselves, the mother always comes to its assistance with an increased interest and gives such instruction and admonition as are useful for the occasion.

It is in this way, and in the use of similar means, that a Christian mother gives her child a proper direction towards the practice of a Christian life, not waiting until it has grown up, but leading it to show itself at once a Christian in all its words and actions. The wholesome influence of instruction such as this cannot be appreciated too highly. There is scarcely anything which offers so sure a pledge that the child will in mature years lead a truly Christian life and arrive at the port of salvation, as its having been instructed from its earliest childhood by its pious mother and taught the practice of faith, hope, charity, and of all the other Christian virtues.

Then, Christian mothers, bestow on your children this inestimable benefit. It will redound to your own joy and consolation.

GOD'S WORD TO THE CHRISTIAN MOTHER.

To give a greater weight to what has been said, it will no doubt be of great help to present the chief passages of Holy Scripture wherein the Holy Ghost addresses Himself to parents.*

1. Let us begin with the words which the Lord spoke to Heli because this high-priest, although he did not entirely neglect the education of his sons, yet by an unreasonable love for them allowed himself to be prevented from punishing them as they merited. These words deserve to be quoted first as showing how earnestly parents should proceed in the education of their children, and the great and strict obligations and responsibilities they are under. They read thus: "Behold, I do a thing in Israel: and whosoever shall hear it, both his ears shall tingle. In that day I will raise up against Heli all

---

* If these passages regard fathers rather than mothers and almost exclusively make mention of sons, it need scarcely be said that they have also the same application to mothers and daughters, since there is no real difference between the duties of the father and of the mother, of the son and of the daughter.

the things I have spoken concerning his house: I will begin, and I will make an end. For I have foretold unto him, that I will judge his house for ever, for iniquity; because he knew that his sons did wickedly and did not chastise them" (I. Kings iii. 11-13). How fully God accomplished what He had prophesied! Both sons of Heli perished during the war; the Ark of the Covenant fell into the hands of the enemy; Heli himself "fell from his stool backwards . . . and broke his neck and died."

2. In the second place, let us mention the beautiful words of the venerable Tobias, a most excellent father, which he pronounced when dying before his equally excellent son and his grandchildren: "Serve the Lord in truth, and seek to do the things that please Him, and command your children that they do justice and alm-deeds, and that they be mindful of God, and bless Him at all times in truth, and with all their power." (Tobias xiv. 10-11.)

3. In the first chapter in the Book of Job is narrated a very touching incident that happened in the family of this great servant of God, and which gives us an insight into

the truly paternal care that their pious father took of his children: "When the days of their feasting were gone about," which his seven sons and three daughters prepared, successively inviting all the others, "Job sent to them and sanctified them"—tried by exhortations and religious ceremonies to move them to contrition and to penance for their sins and to fill them with new fervor—"and rising up early offered holocausts," expiatory sacrifices, "for every one of them. For he said: Lest perhaps my sons have sinned and have blessed God in their hearts"—that is to say, renounced God by having, as it were, dismissed Him. What a beautiful inducement for the Christian mother to offer up prayers and sacrifices for the sins of her children!

4. Holy Scripture teaches also that one of the chief requirements for a good education is goodness and justice on the part of the mother and father. "The just that walketh in his simplicity shall leave behind him blessed children." (Prov. xx. 7.) "A man"—the mother as well as the father—"is known by his children." (Eccl. xi. 30.)

5. Holy Scripture exhorts parents again and again most earnestly to take to heart the proper education of their children. "Instruct thy son, and he shall refresh thee and shall give delight to thy soul." (Prov. xxix. 17.) "Instruct thy son, and labor about him, lest his lewd behaviour be an offence to thee." (Eccl. xxx. 13.) That is to say, take care of his education, else he will degenerate and become a cause of sorrow for thee. "The children of sinners become children of abominations. . . . The inheritance of the children of sinners shall perish." (Ibid. xli. 8, 9.) "Rejoice not in ungodly children, if they be multiplied; neither be delighted in them, if the fear of God be not with them. . . . For better is one that feareth God than a thousand ungodly children. And it is better to die without children than to leave ungodly children." (Eccl. xvi. 1-4.) "A son ill taught is the confusion of the father, and a foolish daughter shall be to his loss. A wise daughter shall bring an inheritance to her husband." (Ibid. xxii. 3.)

6. With great earnestness Holy Scripture warns against that complacency which arises

from a misconceived love or indifference, and which permits children to follow in all things their own will: "Give thy son his way, and he shall make thee afraid: play with him"—that is to say, be wanting in true earnestness in educating him—"and he shall make thee sorrowful." (Eccl. xxx. 9.)

7. Parents must begin early to oppose the faults and bad inclinations of their children. "A horse not broken becometh stubborn, and a child left to himself will become headstrong. . . . Give him not liberty in his youth, and wink not at his devices. Bow down his neck while he is young, and beat his sides while he is a child, lest he grow stubborn and regard thee not, and so be a sorrow of heart to thee." (Ibid. xxx. 8, 11, 12.) "Hast thou children? instruct them, and bow down their neck from their childhood. Hast thou daughters? have a care of their body, and show not thy countenance gay towards them" by laughing extravagantly. (Ibid. vii. 25, 26.)

8. Holy Scripture insists also on strict discipline: "He that loveth his son frequently chastiseth him, that he may rejoice in his latter end." (Eccl. xxx. 1.) "He that spar-

eth the rod hateth his son: but he that loveth him correcteth him betimes." (Prov. xiii. 24.) "The rod and reproof give wisdom: but the child that is left to his own will bringeth his mother to shame." (Ibid. xxix. 15.)

9. To this may be added the admonition of Holy Scripture not to punish in anger and passion: "And you, fathers, provoke not your children to anger"—by angry and passionate expressions—"but bring them up in the discipline and correction of the Lord." (Ephes. vi. 4.) "Fathers, provoke not your children to anger without necessity, lest they be discouraged." (Coloss. iii. 21.)

THE MOTHER OF A PRIEST.

WHAT a blessed vocation is a mother's, and how she rejoices in the elevation and the happiness of her sons! The son obtains an honorable office, he marries into a wealthy and noble family, or he gains some other honorable distinction; what joy for the mother; how happy and contented she feels! and especially if she has reason to say that her son's success can be ascribed to her faithfulness in educating him.

How great, consequently, must not the happiness of a mother be whose son has become a priest of the Most High! For if, with the eye of faith, we consider the dignity of a priest, there can be found none greater here upon earth. It is to be lamented that we judge mostly only by appearances, and that in many priests whom we know the consciousness and dignity of the priestly vocation is perhaps but little apparent. They seem more like common men, and are perhaps no more, not being impressed with the sublimity of their vocation, and not leading lives in accordance with their dignity. Thus it happens that many get only a low conception of the priestly dignity and esteem it but little.

And yet it is as high as heaven. Is a precious gem less precious because he who possesses it does not know its value and cares little about it? Let us look at the priestly dignity in the light of faith and see how sublime it is. Is not the priest in a very high degree the chosen, confidential friend of Jesus Christ, of the Lord and King before whom all knees must bend? Is he not charged with the sublime commission of making men participate in that salvation which He has brought upon earth, the dispensation of which He has confided to His holy Church, giving His priests truly divine powers; among others the power even to change bread and wine into His own flesh and blood, to forgive sins, and to transform sinners into children of God? "O great dignity," exclaims a Saint; "O wonderful power, O sublime office, inspiring men with a holy awe!" "The Lord," thus St. Bernard addresses priests, "has placed you above kings and emperors, above angels and archangels, above all the dominations of heaven." It will only be in heaven, when beholding our Lord Jesus Christ in all His majesty, that we shall learn fully to appreciate the dignity of a priest, that we shall see fully what it is to be a priest—that is to say, a servant and vicar of the Lord of lords.

How great, therefore, will not the honor and majesty of priests be that have lived and died faithful to their high vocation; for at the same time the honorable mark of the priesthood, the indelible sign, will appear in full splendor!

To this must be added the great blessings which go forth from a truly good priest. Let such a priest work as pastor of souls in a parish for a number of years, and the good he will do in the pulpit, in the confessional, at the bedside of the sick, in schools, in families, by word and deed, by example, by prayer, by all his pastoral functions often unseen and unknown, cannot be conceived; it is beyond all calculation. A truly worthy priest and pastor of souls is, in the most beautiful sense of the word, a benefactor of mankind. How great will not one day be his reward! "They shall shine as stars for all eternity."

Can there be, therefore, a greater happiness, looking at things in the light of faith, than to have a son who is called to the great dignity of the priesthood; than to be the mother of a priest? We do not hesitate to apply to her the same words that once were spoken of Mary, the mother of our Lord: "Blessed is the womb that bore thee, and the paps that gave thee suck!" (St. Luke xi. 27.) Blessed be the mother of a priest!

And if the blessing coming from a good priest is so great, will not the mother who has given to the Church a pious priest by the care she took to give her son a truly Christian education also participate in bestowing this blessing, and in its reward?

What joy and consolation will it not be for a mother in heaven to see her son in all the splendor of his priestly dignity, vested in the insignia of the priesthood, raised to a wonderful height of heavenly majesty! But she will also have her part in the reward of all the good which her son has accomplished during his life upon earth, because by piously educating him she has laid the foundation of his priestly piety, and consequently of his successful and blessed pastoral life. "He who receiveth a prophet in the name of the prophet," says our divine Saviour—that is to say, he who receiveth the prophet just because he is a prophet, helping, assisting him to exercise the duties of his vocation, to admonish, to instruct and lead people to salvation—"will receive the reward of a prophet"—that is to say, he will receive a reward similar to that which the prophet himself receives for his labor for the salvation of men, because he has assisted the prophet in them and contributed towards making them successful.

What mother, therefore, will not desire to have a priest among her children, to become the mother of a priest of the Most High! The greater the progress which has been made in true Christian piety, the more one is animated with its spirit, the more clearly will one also realize what has been said of the sublimity of the priestly dignity, and the greater will become the esteem for it. Applying this to a Christian mother, we may say that the greater and more solid her piety is, the more will she desire to become one day the mother of a priest. She must be regarded as lacking in Christian disposition should she never experience such a wish, or should she even dislike and banish from her heart the thought of seeing one of her sons enter the ecclesiastical state.* We could never bring ourselves to consider her a truly Christian mother, however much she might so regard herself and spread abroad the lustre of piety.

* No doubt it would be quite different should there be weighty reasons not incompatible with the principles of our holy religion, for not giving way to such a desire.

The same may be said of the Christian family. A striking characteristic of a Catholic Christian family is love for holy Church. The genuine, faithful Catholic regards her welfare as his own. Full of esteem for her, and ardently desiring that the treasure of salvation prepared by our Lord and confided to her may become more and more diffused among men, he prays unceasingly that the Lord may grant her His powerful assistance. He bears willingly and cheerfully all sacrifices for the fulfilment of this pious desire. And what is there of greater importance for the extension of holy Church than to have good, faithful, and able priests? For this reason holy Church entreats the Lord unceasingly, according to Christ's admonition: "Pray the Lord of the harvest, that he send forth laborers into his harvest." (St. Matt. ix. 38.) And this is one of those things which every good and enlightened Catholic takes most to heart and prays for, seeing what great multitudes are yet wandering "as sheep having no shepherds," and in danger of perishing.

Must not the same also be the object of special solicitude for a Christian mother, supposing her to lead the life of a true, living member of the Church? And how near to her heart, from this point of view, must be the desire that she may be called upon to give up one or the other of her sons to holy Church; to see him one day a priest called to coöperate as a minister of the Church in the accomplishment of her great work? Here, too, it must be added that there is reason to doubt the genuineness, or at least the perfect development, of a true Christian spirit in the mother to whom such wishes and desires are not known.

How often are not such mothers met with, especially in our times! How much the times in which we live tend towards estranging hearts from God and higher things, and towards inducing men to spend all their time and energies in the pursuit of what is merely earthly! How could it be expected that in families wherein such a spirit breathes youthful hearts should be found filled with love, esteem, and inclination for the priesthood, the interests of which are so widely different from those of the world, and very often even disliked and hated by it? This is the cause of the complaint that there is not a sufficient number of priests. Even in Catholic countries, in more than one diocese, the yearly increase of priests no longer corresponds with the necessities of its congregations. And there is ground to fear that those dioceses wherein the want of priests has as yet been less perceptible will soon share the same sad experience. And how sad will be the consequences! Who can number and measure them? What a great misfortune for a congregation of the faithful, especially in our times, if it shall be compelled either to remain without a priest or to enjoy but imperfectly the blessing of a priest's presence!

Is not what has been said of such a nature as to call a Christian mother's attention to her sons? Is it not like a loud voice of supplication which our times, suffering so much from the want of priests, directs to every truly Christian mother, calling upon them to sacrifice their sons for its spiritual necessities?

But—and perhaps the reader has already anticipated this question—supposing even that the thought and desire of seeing her son become a priest may exist in a good

Catholic mother, what will be the use of it? Is it in her power to bring about the fulfilment of her wish?

In answering this question, to which we shall now proceed, we will arrive at the full scope of this treatise. First of all we say briefly: Yes! A mother can do very much towards the accomplishment of this desire.

We do not hesitate to assert that: The very persuasion itself of the great happiness that will flow from having a priest for her son, from being a priest's mother, and the lively desire that such a happiness may fall one day to her lot, furnishes in itself much ground to a Christian mother for hope. Will not this disposition of her heart often urge her to lay her pious desire during prayer before the Lord?

More than once a pious mother has entreated our Lord to give her a son with a vocation to the priesthood, and her prayer has been heard; or, in the hope of being blessed with a son for the priesthood, has already offered him up beforehand to the Lord, and afterwards has not ceased to appear before God frequently in prayer, doing also many other good works in order to obtain this great happiness, and in time the mother's heart has rejoiced at seeing in her son the signs of a priestly vocation.

Let us go on. The child grows up, giving ground for fond hope. Beautiful qualities of mind are united to equally excellent qualities of heart. Besides this a pious and modest disposition develops itself. The mother notices all this with joy. By and by the thought rises in her heart, "May not my son be destined to become a priest? Oh, that he may one day appear at the altar!" Sufficient for her; again and again she recommends her heart's desire to God. Not satisfied with this, she uses every opportunity to present more clearly to her darling, perhaps even jokingly, the idea of becoming a priest.*

---

* She takes, for instance, the little one—we will call him Joseph—to church; there she sees the minister of God at the altar, or in the pulpit, or performing some other priestly function. On reaching home the mother tells what little Joseph has seen in church. "Our Joseph has seen the priest to-day, and he too wishes to become a priest." There are strangers at home who take an interest in the child. "Well, little Joseph," begins the mother, "tell Mr. N. what you wish to become;—he wishes to become a priest." Little Joseph goes to school; he gets a new book. "I declare, when our Joseph becomes a student, how many books he will get then, and how many

It is clear that all this should not be done in a forced or unnatural manner; it should seem to come of itself. Neither should it be done too often, but only occasionally, and in such an easy and natural way that every appearance of persuasion or exhortation may be entirely avoided. For it would be as dangerous as unallowable for a mother, from a rash desire of seeing her son become a priest, to permit herself to persuade him to take such an important step.* If there is in

beautiful things he will learn!" Or he is helped to erect for himself a little altar, a pulpit, and the like; or care is taken that he may learn to serve at Mass, and to assist at the other divine services; or priests are spoken of at home in such a manner as to inspire him with esteem and love for them. Perhaps circumstances may admit of a more familiar intercourse with the priests of the place. They may come from time to time on a visit. The little boy approaches them confidently, he becomes familiar with them. Here are a number of things that may prove to be so many stimulants for the child's inclination to the priesthood. It need not be said that we have mentioned these things only as hints to show how the mother may act with regard to a little son whom she thinks not unfit for the ecclesiastical state, in order to awaken him to a consciousness of his vocation; we have not spoken of the matter at length.

* It would be wholly unallowable, and even criminal, for parents to urge and force their son to enter the priesthood, after having shown himself, either during the

him a true vocation for the priesthood, then, if he be educated in a proper manner, it is easy to call it forth merely by expressions dropped apparently unintentionally.

We say, if he be educated in a proper manner. Here you have what is the most essential of all for a Christian mother to do in order that her son, should he have a true vocation for the priesthood, may follow it and become a priest. The boy, the young man, must be trained by his mother so that he may become animated with a sincere fear of God, and be truly pious. This is indispensably necessary in order that a youth may become conscious of a vocation for the priesthood, and that he may respond to it, that it may be faithfully guarded, and attain maturity. Who can doubt that God, who takes so great care of His holy Church, has given many a youth such a vocation?

But the mothers are wanting to nourish the tender germs of the fear of God planted

course of his studies or at the end of them, totally disinclined to it. In this case they must give up their desire at whatever cost, since by using any kind of coercion to induce their son to become a priest they might become the cause of their son's misfortune as well as of that of many others, and of dishonor to holy Church.

in their hearts. If these do not develop, the noble germ of the priestly vocation also remains undeveloped. It is not made manifest, or at least not as clearly asserted, as it should be. Let us suppose a vocation to the priesthood has really asserted itself, and that the boy has resolved to prepare himself for it. The mother, however, does not know how to educate him in a true and genuine Christian spirit, or has neglected the germs of Christian virtues planted in his heart. The result is, such a boy cannot withstand the bad examples which he meets among the frivolous young men who study with him at the higher schools; he is led into ways of levity and sin, and his vocation often totters, and is even ruined forever. How many times does not this happen! And how often are not the most promising young men in this manner lost to the Church!

Here, then, is another reason for the Christian mother to do with still greater care and interest that which she is already most strictly bound to do; we mean, to make every effort to nourish in her children the spirit of true piety, in order that should a son have a vocation to the priesthood, it may come forth and ripen. And is it not of the first and greatest importance to the priesthood that priests should be truly good and pious? Priests who have a truly priestly heart, who persevere in genuine, solid piety, and who have, with God's grace, from their youth persevered in it—or to speak plainly, those whom a truly Christian mother has inspired from their childhood with the spirit of piety—are exceedingly needed at present. By such our Lord would bring back full salvation to the age in which we live, however much it may seem to have closed itself against it. Oh, the want of true, perfect priestly piety! it is the reason why the endeavors and labors of so many priests remain unblest. Frivolous and wicked priests are the curse, the perdition of the world.

This is the reason, Christian mothers, why our times, and why the Church moved with pity for our times, exhort you thus: "Arise, arise, become mindful of your sublime vocation; bring up truly Christian sons, ground them in true genuine piety, in order that out of their number the army of worthy priests may be recruited! There is need of priests, but there is a still greater need of truly good priests! they alone will bring salvation to the world. This, mothers, this is your sublime vocation! Educate good, worthy priests and give them to the Church; give and present them to the world now so greatly in need of them!"

The call is for you, Christian mother, who are now reading this. Do not turn a deaf ear to it. Foster and cherish in your little sons from their tender years the germs of the fear of God and of piety, especially if you notice in them indications of a vocation to the priesthood. Your breast should exult at the thought, "The Lord has charged me with the education of a priest!" Towards the fulfilment of this charge you must henceforward direct all your powers and energies, according to the instructions we have given.

Recommend unceasingly in your prayers your sons to the Lord with all possible earnestness, especially during holy Mass, and at your holy Communions. Recommend them also to the blessed Virgin Mary, to their guardian angels, to the Saints whose names were given to them in holy baptism, and to all holy priests. Do so above all when any one of them has to leave home to make his preparatory studies for the priesthood at academies and colleges. Ah, what great danger will he not run of there becoming a victim to frivolousness, vices, to a dissolute life, and even of becoming unfaithful to his vocation! Unite, therefore, with the Father in making him firm and strong against such dangers as much as you can ; confide him, if possible, to a good educational institution or to a trustworthy family. But besides all this, never cease to pray with the utmost fervor for him.

THE MOTHER IN HER PRAYER.

A MOTHER who is animated with a truly Christian spirit, and who consequently knows how to value her vocation, will always be much given to prayer. Her very vocation is a continual inducement to seek communion with God. It offers a never-failing nourishment to her spirit. The truly Christian mother is remarkable for her fervor in this exercise. Could it be otherwise? Knowing full well the great responsibility attached to her duties as a mother, and glowing with desire for the happiness of her children, she cannot but feel a never-ceasing impulse to have recourse to God, since it is only by His assistance that she can fulfil these her duties and secure the accomplishment of her motherly desires.

How sublime is the vocation of a mother! How much is required to fulfil all its demands! And how great and numerous the difficulties she has to encounter in the faithful and salutary discharge of her duties. What sacrifices, hardships, and troubles has she not to take upon herself, not only for days, but, if she has many children, for many, many years! Indeed such a task surpasses all human strength. "With man this is impossible." Therefore God must help. It is to Him that the truly good mother has recourse in whatever regards her vocation. She asks of God grace for herself and grace and help for her children. She entreats the Lord to assist her in the discharge of all the duties of her motherhood. She implores His grace to lead a truly Christian life, which is the most essential condition that she may give a good education to her children. She prays for wisdom, that she may discover true God-pleasing ways by which to lead her children to salvation, and especially that she may understand how she should treat each one according to its particular good or bad qualities. She entreats God to give her a true, supernatural, enlightened love for her children, similar to that of the godly Blanche, and to increase such love in her. She prays for courage and strength, for the spirit of self-abnegation and perseverance, that she may not give way to difficulties and troubles which are often very great, and to persevere to the end in all that regards the good education of her children.

It is thus that the mother prays for herself. At one time it is to obtain this grace, at another that. She prays thus in the morning and in the evening, at holy Communion and during other devotions. Perhaps she undertakes from time to time some pious exercises to obtain God's special assistance for the discharge of her duties, and performs for this end some particular good works; above all, works of Christian charity and mercy.

She prays with great confidence, since she knows that the Lord, in the holy Sacrament of Matrimony, and in making her a mother, has given her a right to all those graces which she needs in her vocation, and that He is always ready to grant her as many as are necessary for her true welfare, if she only asks for them in fervent prayer.

And what is the fruit of such prayers? The grace of God shows itself in constantly increasing favors for such a mother. She becomes ever more fit for her vocation, and fulfils its duties in a manner which is a blessing to her children, and for herself a fountain of continual merit. Why is the importance of prayer so little understood by many mothers? They do not pray, and consequently they are not—by their own fault—capable of fulfilling their duties as mothers. Hence so many omissions, so many acts of negligence, so many mistakes and errors in education by which numbers of children are lost.

The mother implores God's grace and assistance also for her children. In the first place, she asks of God to bless whatever she does for her children. She knows full well that whatever she may do for them will not have the desired effect without God's blessing. She is therefore very anxious to accompany whatever she does for her children with a beseeching look to heaven. It is with God that she begins all her work, and to Him she recommends them after having done what was in her power, in order that He may preserve and bless them and make them effective for her children.

The mother prays for her children. God is rich in all good things, and He willingly grants the petition of those who have recourse to Him. Sacred history furnishes abundant examples of mothers who, in consequence of their persevering prayers, have obtained of God the most precious gifts and graces for their children. Have we not also to look here for the reasons why the consolation of seeing their children truly pious and happy is withheld from so many parents? why so many children are given up to bodily and spiritual miseries, and alas! perish miserably? The parents, the mothers, do not pray at all for their children, or not as they should; hence all those gifts and graces which, according to God's holy will, they should receive by the prayers of their parents are withheld from them.

The Christian mother prays for her children. Prayer for her children easily occupies the principal place. She prays that God may preserve them from sin, above all from mortal sin; that He may free them of their faults, that He may give growth and increase to the precious germs of faith, hope, and charity, and to all the other virtues contained in them; that He may lead them to salvation. The truly good mother accompanies her child with prayer to school, to catechism, to confession, and to holy Communion, so that everywhere those endeavors of the child, which of themselves are still insufficient, may by God's blessing become truly beneficial to it.

Let us at this point advance a little beyond the years of childhood. When the child is a prey to bodily infirmities and sufferings, or when the danger of death approaches it, then even less piously-disposed mothers have recourse to prayer; but how much more is this to be expected of a truly Christian mother? But above all does she pray with still greater earnestness and fervor when the souls of her children are exposed to dangers, when there is danger of them falling into mortal sin and of being lost forever. And how great will not her fervor be should she no longer have a personal influence over the child! How anxiously does not her afflicted, oppressed heart then cry to heaven! It was thus that Saint Monica prayed and supplicated for her erring son Augustine during many years and with an abundance of tears; and how glorious was her success!

The world of to-day is, alas! too apt to bring Christian mothers to a similar sad condition. How many sons and daughters are there who, seduced by worldly allurements, have thrown themselves into the arms of frivolity and vice! Ah, if they had mothers like Monica, then there would still be ground for hope. But as the world now moves, they will perish miserably, because their mothers do not know how to pray. To what great dangers are not children exposed, especially when they have to leave home and live with strangers, far from their family,— dangers also which generally grow with increasing age! Behold here another inducement for a Christian mother to multiply her prayers. From that time she will never cease to entreat the Lord to take the son or the daughter under His mighty protection more than ever, that He may restore them to her with their faith and innocence unimpaired.

And the more important the affairs of the children become, the more is Heaven's blessing and protection needed for them, and the greater also will be the mother's fervor and zeal in their behalf.

Thus it happens that the truly Christian mother never grows unaccustomed to the exercise of prayer. Wherever she appears before God in prayer, in the morning or in the evening, in church or at home, at mass, at holy Communion, on Sundays or on feast-days, when making the holy Way of the Cross, on pilgrimages—in short, everywhere her children are present to her mind, they are everywhere the chief object of her prayers and entreaties. And she offers up all her good works, her difficulties, her sufferings, for her children. Her mother's heart gives her no rest until she has performed, especially at stated times, some special good work for their benefit.

It is above all towards Jesus our Lord to whom the devotion of a truly Christian mother for her children is directed, since

He is the Friend of children. She hides her own children in His loving Heart.

She is also active in recommending her children to the prayers of those whom she knows to be consecrated to God, and in whose prayers she thinks she is justified in placing great confidence. Especially does she recommend them to the Saints in heaven, first of all to the blessed Mother of God, then to their guardian angels and to those Saints whose names they bear, and to all the holy and innocent children in heaven.

This is the Christian mother in her prayer! And who can calculate the number of the blessings which the prayers and entreaties of such a pious mother bring down upon the child? The salutary influence of the endeavors of a good mother for her children can scarcely be valued enough; yet her earnest prayers may perhaps do still more for their salvation. This at least cannot be doubted, that without prayer all the efforts of a mother for her children are often entirely useless.

What a powerful motive to pray and to make constant progress in virtue and piety! For the better a mother is the more acceptable are her prayers to God, and the greater and the richer will be the blessings which they will draw down from heaven on her children. In regard to this also the saying is true that "One of the greatest blessings is to have a truly good mother."

Happy, therefore, is the child who is blessed with such a mother! Oh, that we could proclaim throughout the whole world and fix deep in the heart of every mother the words, "Pray; pray without ceasing; pray with all earnestness and fervor for your children!"

PART II.

Prayers for a Christian Mother.

It is a beautiful and commendable practice, to read in the afternoons of Sundays, if it be only during the devotion—but not during the prayers, that may perhaps be said in common—one of the chapters of the first part, either entirely or partly. By this, what has been said would always be called to mind.

PRAYERS FOR THE MOST IMPORTANT SITUATIONS AND NECESSITIES OF A MOTHER.

*Prayer on the Anniversary of her Marriage.**

O my God and my Lord, it was on this day that I knelt in Thy holy house at the nuptial altar, that I received the sacrament of matrimony and entered with Thy blessing the matrimonial state. Can I let this day pass without giving thanks to Thee and without some special exercise of piety? No, O Lord! I thank Thee, therefore, from my

* Good Christians thus happily united should approach together the sacraments, either on the anniversary of their marriage or on the Sunday preceding or following it, in order to receive them with better preparation, and to renew the graces of the sacrament of matrimony. What a beautiful practice! Could not married people at least assist at Mass with this intention? Do they realize how much they stand in need of the blessing and assistance of God in the midst of so many important duties, surrounded as they are by so many difficulties and dangers, that they may not perish, but work out their salvation? It was for this very reason that our Lord instituted the sacrament of matrimony, and this same reason shows also how commendable a practice it is to renew yearly the graces received in this Sacrament.

heart, for having introduced me by a holy sacrament into the state of matrimony, for having sanctified my matrimonial union, for having opened to me the treasures of Thy graces, that I might be enabled to live up to the duties of my vocation, to persevere in inviolable fidelity, in love, and in dutiful submission to my husband, and in the chastity conformable to my state of life, and to educate the children whom Thou hast confided to me in Thy fear and discipline, and thus work out my eternal salvation. I give Thee thanks for all the graces which I have received in virtue of this sacrament. I thank Thee for the protection, the assistance, and for whatever good Thou hast bestowed upon me and upon my family. Be Thou for all these eternally praised and blessed!

But have I faithfully coöperated with Thy grace in fulfilling the duties of my vocation? Have I led the life of a truly Christian wife? Alas! too much have I to reproach myself with. [*Here reflect a little while.*] O my God, I am sorry from my heart for having offended Thee. Pardon me for the sake of Thy infinite mercy and for that of Jesus, Thy beloved Son! My resolution is firmly taken. I will endeavor to fulfil henceforward all the duties of a Christian wife and mother faithfully and conscientiously. How could I otherwise hope to enjoy Thy grace and to work out my salvation? But what will all my good resolutions avail me if Thou dost not give Thy help to fulfil them? Renew then, O Lord, on this day the blessing of this holy sacrament; may its graces flow upon me in abundance every day. Animated and strengthened by them I will try in the future to lead a life in harmony with my vocation.

I recommend to Thee also my husband. Grant that we who are by virtue of this sacrament so intimately united may live always in heartfelt love and in true fear of God, in order that our matrimonial state may, as it should be, a symbol of that intimate union existing between Christ and His holy Church and lead us to life eternal.

I commend unto Thee also, O Lord, the children whom Thou hast confided to our care. Bless them, protect them, enrich them with Thy graces, that they may grow up pleasing to Thee. Assist me to educate them wholly for Thee. Holy Virgin and

Mother of God, holy Joseph and all ye who have led a holy life in the state of matrimony, all ye holy parents, pray for me. Amen.

Prayer for the First Visit to Church.

I give thanks to Thee, O God! that by Thy goodness I am permitted to appear again in Thy holy house. I give Thee thanks for the protection and assistance with which Thou hast favored me. I thank Thee especially for all the happiness, the joy I experience at Thy hands in the gift of my child. It is Thy gift. Thou hast made it in the sacrament of regeneration Thy own child. Thou hast invested it with all the distinctions of Thy children, and hast opened to it all the treasures of Thy holy Church, yes, all the riches of the majesty of heaven, with a prospect of the highest, an eternal happiness.

O my God! infinitely merciful, loving, and full of bounty, be Thou blessed and praised for all Thou hast done for my child. Thou hast given it to me, that I may henceforward fulfil towards it all the duties of a Christian mother, and by doing so, educate my child for Thee and for heaven.

My heart is ready, O Lord! my heart is

ready; but how shall I fulfil these manifold and difficult duties of a mother if Thou dost not assist me with Thy grace? Assist me then. Fill my heart with Thy holy Spirit; give me zeal, wisdom, and strength, that I may accomplish the important work of education, according to Thy holy will and for the salvation of my child and of myself.

In union with the holy Mother of my Lord, and with the same sentiments with which she offered up herself and her Divine Child in the temple, I this day offer up myself and my child to Thee, O God! Graciously grant that my child, being now also Thy child, may forever remain Thine; may I henceforward live only to guard my child and lead it to Thee! Holy Virgin Mary, beloved Mother of my God! with what sentiments of thankfulness and loving reverence didst Thou not offer up Thy Divine Child in the temple! I unite myself to Thee, and I recommend my child and all that I shall do henceforward for it to Thy powerful intercession. Amen.*

* How beautiful if on this occasion, too, the mother would assist at Mass, giving thanks to God and laying before Him her necessities!

Prayer in the Morning.

Most merciful God! Thou hast given me this day, that I may serve Thee and work out my salvation by the faithful discharge of my duties. Assist me then with Thy grace! Above all, assist me that I may fulfil to-day the most important and most sacred duties which I owe to my children with care and fidelity, and especially that I may go before them with the light of good example. Bless whatever I may do or say on this day for their education.

Take, O God! my children under the protection of Thy love and grace. Shield them from danger, and keep them far from all evil! Preserve them from sin! Fill their tender hearts with Thy holy love! Awake and incite them with Thy grace, that they may serve Thee faithfully, and grow in virtue and grace before Thee as they grow in age. To you, holy guardian angels, and to you, Saints in heaven whose names my children bear, I recommend them; take care of them, pray for them. Amen.

*Prayer in the Evening.**

Thanks be to Thee, O my God and Father! for all the graces and favors which Thou hast graciously bestowed to-day upon me and upon my children. All good gifts proceed from Thee. Thou rulest over us with mercy. Woe to me, that I am so ungrateful and have so often offended Thee, the best of Fathers! Mercifully pardon me, especially for the sins which as a mother I have

---

* Do not omit, Christian mother, to examine your conscience in the evening, if it be only for some minutes, especially whether you have faithfully performed your duties during the day. Was your example such as to be worthy of imitation? Have you said or done anything that could have given scandal to your children? Have you had as careful an eye over your children as you should have had? Have you permitted them to rove about unguarded? Have you brought them to church, to school? Did you take it to heart to give them useful instruction; to remind them of God, and of higher things? Have you reminded them of their faults? Have you admonished, warned. and punished them according to duty? Have you, in doing this, given way to anger and impatience, and punished them beyond measure? Have you taught them to say their prayers and insisted on their doing so; on their loving God and man; on their being truthful, obedient, peaceable, industrious, lovers of cleanliness and order? Do you pray for them as you should? Be sorry if you have committed faults; ask God's pardon, resolve and promise our Lord to be more faithful on the morrow.

this day committed! . . . What can I do, except to ask for mercy? Be Thou merciful unto me! Oh, that I may recognize more and more the sanctity of my vocation, and fulfil its duties perfectly! Yes, O Lord, I have resolved to do so. I renew my promise to Thee. Hasten to help me with the riches of Thy grace. Inflame my heart more and more with Thy holy love, and with true charity for my children, so that I may be always filled with holy earnestness in the education of my children, and in whatever regards their true welfare.

Father, I commend to Thee my children during this night. May Thy hand defend them during their night's rest; drive far away from their place of rest the enemy of men; let their holy angels be near to them. Do not permit the night to become for them an occasion of sin; preserve them in innocence and unsullied purity! Holy Virgin, St. Joseph, ye holy angels, and all ye Saints in heaven, I recommend my children to you. Amen.

PRAYER OF A CHRISTIAN MOTHER AT HOLY MASS.*

For Herself to obtain Graces necessary to fulfil the Duties of her Vocation.

AT THE INTROIT OF THE MASS.

O my God! I appear here in Thy holy temple to ask grace and help to fulfil the duties of my vocation. I cannot perform

---

* The greater the necessities of a mother, the greater are the graces she stands in need of to enable her to discharge her duties, and the more anxious she should be to have frequent recourse to the holy sacrifice of the Mass. During Mass she stands not alone before the Lord, although from her poverty, indigence, and unworthiness she might seem to be in great danger of not being looked upon with favor. When she comes to thank God, either for herself or for her children, or to ask for new favors, if approaching with faith and confidence, Jesus will step in her place by the great sacrifice of Himself, offering Himself up for her and for her children to the heavenly Father as a sacrifice of thankfulness and prayer, since she herself may take this holy sacrifice and (offering it up to heaven) present it as her own to the justice and mercy of God. Oh, what a blessing for mother and children! Would to God that all mothers valued this blessing sufficiently! How beautiful a sight would be offered to angels and to men if a mother, whenever possible, would assist at the holy sacrifice of Mass with the intention of obtaining all those graces she stands in need of for the good and perfect edu-

these duties according to Thy holy will and for the benefit of my children without Thy special help. Thou hast promised me the especial assistance of Thy grace in the holy sacrament of matrimony. Oh that I may become more worthy of it! O my God! I am fully aware of my unworthiness to receive Thy gracious assistance. I come, therefore, to the altar of Thy divine Son in order that

---

cation of her children, or with the intention that God might give success to whatever she or the father, the priest and teachers do for her children, or to commend them to the special care and protection of God, or to ask of Him a particular help which the one or the other of her children may at the time stand in need of, either to free itself from a bad habit or to perform well an important action—for example, to go to school, to confession, to receive for the first time holy Communion, to leave home, and the like. Certainly this would be highly pleasing to God, it would be according to His holy desire; it would open the fountain of graces contained in the holy sacrifice, and would bring its salutary effects into the family for the salvation of parents and children. Could any one give a greater consolation to our Lord, the friend of children, than a Christian mother, who is present at holy Mass in behalf of her children? For this reason you find here a number of prayers adapted to the most common necessities of a mother. These prayers can also be said at any time, but hardly at any time better than during the holy sacrifice, inserting them between the other prayers for Mass, either in the beginning or during the Canon, or after consecration.

I may, in union with this holy sacrifice which He offers up to Thee also for me, appear not wholly unworthy to be heard when imploring Thy divine assistance in my vocation and Thy grace for my children. Grant that I may assist at this holy sacrifice with true devotion and return from it laden with Thy heavenly blessings. Amen.

AT THE OFFERTORY.*

Almighty and eternal God, in union with the priest, I offer to Thee these gifts of bread and wine, and with them I desire to present the petitions of my heart, my earnest request for grace to fulfil my duties. In spirit I lay them on the altar before Thee, O my God! I know that like the bread and wine, so also my prayers are of little or no value before Thee; but as through Thy goodness and power bread and wine are changed into the infinitely pleasing sacrifice of the precious body and blood of Thy divine Son, so grant that, in union with the holy sacrifice, my petitions may find before Thee grace and fulfilment. I entreat Thee, therefore, in the

* In the mean time, especially at the Canon and after consecration, the prayers, page 175, may be said.

spirit of humility and with a heart filled with contrition, invoking, at the same time, the intercession of the most blessed Virgin Mary, St. Joseph, all holy mothers, and all the Saints in heaven. Amen.

AT THE CONSECRATION.

O Jesus, Thou deignest to descend again with infinite love at the word of Thy minister upon the altar, to represent, under the appearances of bread and wine, that merciful and gracious sacrifice which Thou hast offered up on Golgotha in order to make us participate in its infinite blessings. With the most profound humility I adore Thee, my Lord and Saviour, now mercifully present upon the altar. I praise Thee and thank Thee from the depth of my heart for Thy infinite goodness and mercies. Receive, O my Jesus, my petitions, and grant them through Thy merits, so that I may be to the children, whom Thou lovest so tenderly, a truly good mother. Amen.

AFTER THE CONSECRATION.

O my God! my heart rises now with hope and confidence toward Thee, for it is Thy divine Son who takes my place and lays my petitions before Thee, in union with the sacrifice of His sacred flesh and blood. It is the same sacrifice that He once offered up on the cross, being obedient unto death, and which is infinitely pleasing to Thee. May my prayers, in union with this holy sacrifice and through it, find grace before Thee. Pardon me my transgressions in the discharge of the duties of my vocation, and grant that I may fulfil them with renewed fervor from this day. Grant me all I need for the education of my children, to lead an exemplary life, the spirit of true love and charity, heavenly wisdom, perseverance in patience, mildness, zeal and fervor in prayer for my children. Enable me to educate them in such a manner that their education may redound to Thy honor and their salvation, as well as the salvation of my own soul. Amen.

Our Father, etc.

BEFORE AND AT COMMUNION.

Prayer to Jesus, the friend of children, page 182.

AT THE END OF MASS.

Prayer to the Holy Ghost to obtain His sevenfold gifts, page 184, and the prayers, page 186.

Prayers for a Mother who assists at Mass for the Benefit of her Children.

AT THE INTROIT.

O my God! the love of my children and the desire for their salvation leads me to-day to Thy holy altar, and to the sacrifice of Thy divine Son. However great the desire of my heart for my children's welfare may be, however much I may endeavor to educate them well, all my endeavors will remain without success, and without true blessings, if Thou withhold Thy assistance and help from my children. I entreat Thee, therefore, to come to my help. And since my prayers and entreaties are of themselves unworthy of being laid before Thee, I unite them with this holy sacrifice of Thy divine Son, my Lord, and I offer up this holy sacrifice for my children. Give me grace that I may do it with true devotion, and may obtain for my dear children heavenly blessings. Amen.*

AT THE OFFERTORY.

The poor gifts of bread and wine are offered up to Thee by the priest in order

---

* Prayers at page 189-219 may be inserted.

that Thou mayest Thyself prepare out of them a sacrifice pleasing to Thee. The moment draws near when by the words of the priest, pronounced by him in the name of our divine Saviour, the wonderful transubstantiation will take place, in consequence of which Thy divine Son will be our High Priest and Sacrifice. Lead, then, my children in spirit to this hallowed spot, that the blessing of this sacrifice may descend in great abundance upon them. Let them through the merits of this holy sacrifice obtain pardon of their sins and grace to avoid them for the future. As by Thy divine power bread and wine are changed into the most sacred flesh and blood of Jesus Christ, show also in virtue of this holy sacrifice the power of Thy grace on my children, that their hearts may become changed more and more into perfect models of Christian piety, and thus become a pleasing sacrifice in Thy sight. Remember that they are also Thy children. Therefore bless them with Thy graces, that they may become worthy of Thee. Grant that they may adhere to Thee with a lively faith, and with the love of children, and may make Thy holy will the rule of their life, and never depart from it, so that, walking in Thy holy ways, they may be happy for time and eternity. Amen. Ye Saints of God, holy Virgin Mary, Saint Joseph, holy guardian angels, and all ye holy children, assist, help me in my prayers, and entreat God that the fruit of this holy sacrifice may flow down in abundance upon my children. Amen.

AT THE CONSECRATION.

My divine Saviour, who didst once go about among men, enriching them with all kinds of blessings and graces: Thou art now again near to me, having taken once more Thy abode among the children of men under the mysterious appearances of bread and wine. Again dost Thou offer Thyself up to Thy heavenly Father upon the altar. Like the mothers who lived with Thee in the Holy Land, I too will use these sacred moments, and lead my little ones in spirit to Thee. O Lord Jesus, all the graces and blessings Thou didst bestow on the children of those mothers, whilst folding them in Thy arms and laying Thy hands on them, graciously bestow through this holy sacrifice upon my children also. Amen.

AFTER THE CONSECRATION.

O God, heavenly Father, as Thou didst formerly behold Thy Son from heaven, and spoke to Him, saying, "This is my beloved Son, in whom I am well pleased," whilst he wandered about and labored here upon earth, so now Thou also lookest down upon Him with complacency, whilst He renews mysteriously His holy sacrifice for the honor of Thy holy name and for the welfare of Thy children. Uniting, therefore, in the holy sacrifice, I appear with confidence before the throne of Thy mercy, to recommend my children to Thee. Let them experience Thy powerful protection in all dangers of soul and body. Keep them far from sin and whatever may cause injury to their souls. Direct graciously all their temporal concerns for the best. Keep them in unblemished innocence, and preserve them in Thy grace! Grant that they may increase according to the example of our divine Saviour, in true wisdom as in age, in virtue and in grace before God and man. O God! powerful in thy grace, be Thou, by the virtue of this holy sacrifice of Thy Son, in such a manner with my children that they may also be my consolation and my joy here upon earth and my crown in eternity, and that Thou, O great Father, mayest have complacency on them as on Thy beloved children. Amen.

Our Father, for the children.

AT HOLY COMMUNION.

O Lord Jesus Christ, Son of the living God, once more I have recourse to Thee. According to the will of Thy Father, and with the coöperation of the Holy Ghost, by Thy death Thou hast brought life to the world. I entreat Thee, therefore, through this Thy most sacred flesh and blood, to deliver my children from all their transgressions and from all evil, and grant that they may always keep firmly Thy holy commandments, and never be separated from Thee. Amen.

AT THE END OF MASS.

Prayer, pages 189, etc.

DIFFERENT PRAYERS FOR THE USE OF THE CHRISTIAN MOTHER.

FOR HERSELF.

Prayer to obtain the Grace to give Good Example.

O GOD, what a powerful exhortation Thy divine Son addresses to me also when He says, "Let your light shine." It is Thy holy will that I should give to my children in all things the example of a life pleasing to Thee. How else can they become virtuous themselves? I ask, therefore, for Thy assistance, through the merits of this holy sacrifice, to lead a truly Christian life. Enrich me with Thy grace, that I may be able to avoid in all my words, actions, and omissions what is unworthy of the name of Christian. Help me to exercise all the virtues of a Christian life, and to arrive at ever-increasing perfection, so that my life may be an example for my children.

How wonderfully, O Lord, hast Thou worked in Thy Saints! Watch over and graciously protect me. I am indeed not worthy of such great graces; but Thou art a merciful God; Thou lovest my children, since they are also Thy children. For their sake and that of Jesus, Thy Son, grant my petitions. Amen.

Prayer to obtain True Supernatural Love for her Children.

My God, and Father of my children, since Thou hast confided them to me, Thou hast given to my heart a share of that love which Thy divine heart bears to them, and Thou art ready, in virtue of the holy sacrament of matrimony, to purify and elevate this natural love of a mother by Thy grace, so that it may become like Thy love, for the great benefit of my children. I implore Thee, relying upon the virtue of this holy Sacrament, through the merits of Thy divine Son, through His love for children, and through the intercession of all holy mothers, that I may be blessed with this grace. Do not allow that, blinded by mere natural love, I should neglect what is required for the good and Christian education of my children! Guard me against untimely indulgence and forbearance! Give me strength and courage that I may not fear to chastise, when necessity requires, according to duty and in the right spirit.

Enlighten me, O God! that, looking at my children with the eye of Faith, I may learn to love them more and more with that love which Thou bearest to them; that, clothed with sanctifying grace, I may love them as Thy children; that I may love them as brothers and sisters of Jesus Christ, and as temples of the Holy Ghost regard them as members of that holy communion of Saints who are called to behold Thy majesty and participate in thy happiness forever.

Grant then, O God! that by the consideration of these truths and by the power of Thy grace the sacred love of my children may become perfect in me; that it may be my greatest concern at all times to educate them more and more as children worthy of Thee, and in true and filial fear of Thee and piety, so that they may glorify Thy holy name to the end and be saved. Fill me with zeal for the salvation of their souls! Awaken and strengthen me, so that no pains may be too great for me, no sacrifice too heavy, and that I may persevere unshaken in working, suffering, praying for the salvation of my children. My Lord, give me that holy love wherewith Thou hast filled the hearts of so many holy mothers, through Jesus Christ. Amen.

Prayer to obtain True Wisdom.*

O my God! how great and how important is the vocation which Thou hast given me, and how difficult its duties! I am called to educate the children whom Thou hast confided to me, each of them according to its

---

* " And Solomon loved the Lord, walking in the precepts of David his father, . . . and the Lord appeared to Solomon in a dream by night, saying, ' Ask what thou wilt that I should give thee.' And Solomon said, ' Thou hast shown great mercy to Thy servant David, my father. . . . And now, O Lord, Thou hast made Thy servant a king instead of David, my father; and I am but a child, and know not how to go out and come in. . . . Give, therefore, to thy servant an understanding heart, to judge Thy people and discern between good and evil. For who shall be able to judge this people, Thy people which is so numerous?' And the word was pleasing to the Lord that Solomon had asked such a thing. And the Lord said to Solomon, ' Because thou hast asked this thing, and hast not asked for thyself long life nor riches, nor the lives of thy enemies, but hast asked for thyself wisdom to discern judgment, behold I have done for thee according to thy words, and have given thee a wise and understanding heart.'" What a motive, what an exhortation for a Christian mother to make a similar petition! Will not the Lord hear her?

peculiar character; and to induce them to rid themselves of their faults, and to practise Christian virtues. O my God! I am ignorant and weak. How will I be able to see always the way that leads to success without Thy assistance? Send down, O Lord of light and knowledge, a ray of Thy divine wisdom from Thy heavenly throne into my heart as Thou didst once give to Solomon, in answer to his prayer, a wise and intelligent heart, so that he was enabled to govern his people. Enlighten me that I may understand how I must treat my children according to each one's character, so that they may be freed from their faults and remain preserved from what is injurious and dangerous to them. Show me the ways and means to educate them; guide me that I may keep equally far from undue severity and from untimely indulgence. Inspire me with the proper spirit to reprehend, to mistrust, and to admonish them. Grant me the blessing to fulfil my duties led, as it were, by Thy hand, which leads all Thy children with infinite wisdom in the way which is best for their salvation. O Holy Ghost! Thou who bestowest infinite graces,

grant me the gift of wisdom and counsel for the benefit of my children. Amen.
Our Father and *Hail Mary.*

Prayer for the Gift of Fortitude.

O God! Thou knowest how easily I become disheartened and impatient at the necessities, privations, and exertions which the education of children requires of me. And woe to me should I allow myself to be induced by them to omit or to neglect what I must do for their welfare! Grant unto me, therefore, courage and strength, so that I may willingly take upon myself these difficulties and sacrifices of my vocation and bear them with patience. Teach me to venerate in them the Cross, which Thy holy will has laid upon me for my salvation, so that I may take it up daily and follow my Saviour, who has done and suffered far more for me. Turn my eyes towards the precious reward of so many pains and difficulties, which will further the salvation of my children, and obtain for myself untold bliss in heaven. Grant, then, that I may always perform for my children, without fear of labor and privations, whatever is nec-

essary for and conducive to their good education. O Holy Ghost, spirit of strength, grant me the gift of fortitude! Amen.
Our Father and *Hail Mary.*

Prayer for the Spirit of Mildness.

O divine Saviour, who didst converse with Thy Apostles for three years as a father with his children, how much didst Thou not suffer from their wretchedness, from their imperfections and faults, and how often was not their behavior such as should have called forth Thy just anger and indignation! And yet how full of indulgence and condescension Thou wast always for them! No unkind or harsh word ever passed Thy lips. Oh, that I might be like Thee in my behavior toward my children! I must be so if I wish to be Thy disciple and work out my salvation. Let me learn of Thee to be mild of heart. When anger and impatience arise in me at the ill behavior of my children, help me to overcome these emotions. Grant me grace to conquer myself, so that I may remain quiet and discreet whenever I have to reprehend or punish; for anger does not work what is just in Thy sight. O most mild Jesus, have mercy on me! Amen.*

Prayer to Jesus, the Friend of Children.†
Especially to be said during Mass, at Holy Communion, or at other times before the Blessed Sacrament.

O Jesus, how great was once Thy love for children! Is it as great to-day? Yes. Thy love for Christian children is even greater. Thou lovest also my children, divine Saviour, more than I love them myself. Thou art

---

* The more a mother is inclined to anger, and the more easily she is carried away by it, the more firmly must she resolve to be on her guard, and the more fervently should she ask of our Lord His assistance, not only in the morning, but also at other times, that she may thus learn to master her anger, one of the greatest vices in a mother.

† "At one time," as we read in the Gospel, St. Mark chap. x. 13-16, "little children were brought to Jesus" by their mothers "that He might touch them with His hand. And the disciples," who wished to spare their Master, who was already so much molested, this new trouble, "rebuked those that brought them. But when Jesus saw it He was much displeased, and said to them, 'Suffer little children to come to me, and forbid them not: for of such is the kingdom of God.' And embracing them, and laying His hands upon them, he blessed them." Could He have made known His love in a more touching manner? Similar instances of His love for children are related in the Gospel in other places. And have we no reason to believe that our Lord loves Christian children still more?

their divine Friend. Oh, how consoling and encouraging for me! Be Thou praised and extolled for this. Grant me, O divine Saviour, the grace that I may in all things behave and act with regard to my children as will be pleasing to Thy divine heart. Grant me to educate them entirely for Thee, and to make every effort that they may increase in the knowledge of Thee, love Thee daily more and more, and live always according to the example of Thy holy life, so that they may be Thy true disciples, and obtain through Thee their salvation. O my Jesus, in virtue of the holy sacrament by which Thou hast introduced me into the state of matrimony and called me to be a mother, and through the graces of Thy holy sacrifice enable me to fulfil most faithfully and zealously all the duties of a Christian mother! Let my life be a model for my children; penetrate my heart with that love which Thy divine heart bears for my children; give me wisdom, give me fortitude, give me patience and mildness, give me fervor in prayer. May Thy divine blessing be bestowed upon all I do for my children! Amen.

Prayer to the Holy Ghost for His Seven Gifts.

O Holy Ghost! Fountain-head and dispenser of all graces and gifts, I have recourse to Thee. How much do I not stand in need of Thy gifts in my work of education! Grant these to me in ever-increasing plenitude!

Grant me the gift of wisdom, that in educating my children I may intend, above all else, the welfare of their souls, and recognize in all things what are the best ways and means to lead them to the true fear of God and piety, and to their salvation. Amen.

Give me the gift of understanding, in order that, led by Thee to the right comprehension of the teachings of our holy religion, I also may be able to instruct my children properly, and obtain for them a heartfelt, sincere religious spirit. Amen.

Give me the gift of knowledge, that I may know and see what is conducive to my own and my children's welfare, and become thus enabled to communicate to them the most necessary and most useful knowledge in whatever they have a right to be instructed in by me. Amen.

Give me the gift of counsel, that in the

difficult task of education I may always find the right way, use the right means, and proceed in the best manner to do for my children all that is according to God's holy will, and for their true welfare. Amen.

Give me the gift of fortitude, that I may not fail under the difficulties and privations of a mother; but persevere with a cheerful and joyful heart, that I may never permit myself to give way to undue love for my children, which would bring upon them the loss and ruin of their souls. Amen.*

Give me the gift of piety, and kindle in my heart, by Thy grace, the fire of holy love, that by my faithfulness in the service of God, and by my zeal in the practice of Christian piety and Christian virtues, I may set before my children the example of a perfect Christian life, and that my teaching and admonitions may thus, by the unction of the true fear of God and by Thy holy grace, become fruitful for them. Amen.

Give me the gift of the fear of the Lord,

---

* If time permits, after each of these prayers one *Our Father* and one *Hail Mary* should be said, adding after the word Jesus: " Who will bestow on me the gift of wisdom, understanding, knowledge."

and penetrate my heart with hatred and aversion for sin, and with a holy abhorrence for all that may be displeasing in Thy sight, that I may not by my sins give scandal to my children and become the cause of sir and the perdition following it—the greatest misfortune that could befall them. Amen.

Prayer to the Blessed Virgin Mary.

O most blessed Virgin Mary, admirable Mother, I fly to Thee, since I am called b' the Lord to be a mother. Oh, that I might also as mother resemble Thee, and be not unworthy of Thy love! Obtain for me, C holy and mighty mother, this grace. May it be granted to me, through Thy powerful intercession, to fulfil always faithfully, conscientiously, and perseveringly all the duties which I have to fulfil as a Christian mother! What a pleasing, holy life was that which Thou, O holy Mother, didst lead at the side of Thy holy spouse with Jesus, Thy divine Son, in the humble dwelling of Nazareth! Oh, let it be the model of my life! Pray that the spirit of the fear of God and piety may descend upon our home, so that my children may thrive and prosper in all that is good and pleasing to God! Amen.

*Prayer to St. Joseph.**

St. Joseph, faithful companion of the holy Mother of God, Thy Virgin-spouse, whom together with her Divine Child thou hast guarded with such great care and devotion, and to whom Thou hast sacrificed Thy whole life, I entreat thee to be also my guardian and intercessor with Jesus, Thy most noble foster-son. Obtain for me the grace that I may fulfil my duties to my children as Thou with Thy holy spouse didst fulfil thy duties toward Jesus. Blessed Joseph, pray for me! Amen.

Prayer to the Guardian Angels.†

O holy Guardian Angels, heavenly friends of my children, I address myself with confidence to You, as the children whom the Lord has confided to me are also looked

---

* Would to God that all parents, as the holy Virgin, were also devout to St. Joseph, and would venerate Him as the Patron of Christian families!

† According to the doctrine of holy Church, the belief that children are assisted by holy Guardian Angels is well founded. Should it not inspire mothers with a special veneration for the Guardian Angels of their children? Is it not appropriate to regard them as friends of the house, to venerate them, and consequently to have especial recourse to them in all that concerns the children?

upon by You with love and care. Implore for me the grace that I may cherish for my children sentiments similar to those which You have for them, and that I may, like You, be anxious above all to educate them for God and for heaven. Oh, that I may be such a mother to my children ; that I may never appear unworthy of Your love and friendship! Obtain this grace for me. Amen.

*Prayer to the Saints whose Names the Children bear.**

Holy patrons of my children, holy . . . extend Your care also to me, their mother; pray for me, that I may obtain, by Your intercession, the grace to exercise in word and deed a wholesome influence over my children, so that they may grow up in faithful imitation of Your virtues, as truly good members of holy Church, and be one day received into Your blessed society. Amen.

* They too should be justly venerated and invoked, since they have in holy baptism been appointed, to be not only models for imitation, but also intercessors of the children. Hence also the direction of holy Church to give to the children not profane names, but the names of *Saints.*

For the Children.

Prayer of the Mother to obtain God's Blessing on the labors she undergoes for her Children.

O my God, I know too well that whatever I may do for the education of my children will remain fruitless without the blessing of Thy grace. "Unless the Lord build the house," says the psalmist, "they labor in vain who build it. Unless the Lord keep the city, he watcheth in vain that keepeth it." (Ps. 126.) I pray to Thee, therefore, O Lord, to give success to what I do for my children. Grant that they may remain preserved from all evil of body and soul, help me build so that the edifice of virtue and perfection may have in them a firm, solid foundation and rise higher and higher; graciously accompany all my words and actions with Thy grace, so that whatever I say and do may tend to their true welfare. Through Jesus Christ our Lord. Amen.

Prayer for the Protection of the Children in all their Dangers.

O my God, to how many and to what great dangers are my children not exposed, and how insufficient is the protection that I can afford them! Yes, O Lord, I watch in vain over them if Thou dost not watch with me. But when they abide under Thy protection, how secure may I not be! I recommend, therefore, my children to Thy powerful and loving care. Keep graciously far from them all that may prove hurtful and dangerous to their life; let them enjoy the blessing of health; but, above all, protect them in the dangers of their souls. Drive away from them with Thy powerful hand whatever may have an injurious influence upon their yet tender and youthful hearts and become for them an occasion of wickedness and sin! Send Thy holy angels, that they may "bear them up in their hands, lest they should dash their feet against a stone." Almighty Father, lead my children through the dangers and storms of this life, so that they may arrive one day at the haven of salvation. Amen.

Prayer that The Lord may preserve the Children from Grievous Sin.

O my God, how numerous and how great are the dangers of sin and corruption that beset my children! Alas! I will never be able to shelter them sufficiently against these dangers. Thou must come to my assistance; Thou must lead them to victory. Come then, O Lord, with the power of Thy grace and hasten to their help, with the fulness of Thy strength, in order that the monster of mortal sin may not come near to any of them. Thou knowest, O Lord, how much I love them; yet I would prefer to lose them by death rather than they should fall into mortal sin, and thus lose the life of their souls and incur Thy displeasure and hatred. I therefore implore Thee, Father of my children, hasten to take them out of this life, if living longer here on earth should plunge them into the greatest of all misfortunes! Grant, I beseech Thee, that I may meet them, after this short stay upon earth, in Thy heavenly home. Listen to me, O Lord, and grant my petition, through Jesus Christ our Lord. Amen.

Ave Maria.

Prayer to obtain for the Children the Grace of the True Fear of God.

O God! "every good gift proceedeth from Thee." It is only through Thee that we are able to think anything truly good. Thou workest the willing and perfecting of all that is good. In holy baptism Thou hast made my children Thy children, and hast planted in their hearts the germs of virtue. Their growth and development is also Thy work. Grant that they may always live and act according to the teachings of their holy faith. Raise their hearts to heavenly thoughts and desires. Enkindle in them the fire of Thy holy love, that they may adhere to Thee, keep always before their eyes and fulfil always faithfully Thy holy commandments. Nourish in them the spirit of prayer, that they may be zealous in the performance of their spiritual exercises and, in frequenting divine service, may learn how to pray well and become rich in heavenly graces. Preserve them in unblemished innocence and purity of heart. Thou art powerful, O God, to bestow all gifts in abundance. Visit, then, my children with Thy grace, so that they may become firmly rooted in sincere piety and fear of God, increase therein, and attain their salvation. Amen.

Prayer to obtain for the Children Grace to fulfil the Duties of their State of Life.

All-merciful God! give to my children the grace to fulfil, conscientiously and faithfully, all those duties which they owe to their parents. It is Thy holy will that every one should serve Thee above all, and chiefly, by the faithful fulfilment of the duties of his state of life. Thou requirest, therefore, of my children nothing more rigorously than to behave to their parents with respect, love, and submission. It is only by doing this that they can please Thee. Inspire, O mildest of Fathers, my children with sentiments of respect and love; inspire them always to meet their parents respectfully, and submit themselves willingly and cheerfully to them in all things. Mortify their wilfulness and stubbornness; teach them to obey willingly and cheerfully all the orders of their parents. Thou hast added to the faithful fulfilment of the Fourth Commandment a great blessing for eternity. Let this blessing, O Lord, descend in abundance upon my children! Amen.

Prayer to obtain for the Children the Virtue of Chastity.

O Most Holy God! who lovest purity and innocence, grant to my children the precious gift of purity. Woe to them should the vice of impurity take hold of their hearts! How miserable would they not be! O Lord, do Thou guard them! Keep with Thy powerful hand this monster far from them. Without Thy special help they cannot preserve the virtue of chastity. O God, grant them this help. By it let their hearts be like sanctuaries, unprofaned, undefiled by any impure thought or feeling; by it let their eyes be modest, bashful; their ears and mouth unapproachable, and closed to any impropriety in word and deed. By Thy grace fill them with hatred against whatever may be contrary to decency, and let them persevere, body and soul, in unimpaired purity, so that they may always stretch out to Thee pure hands, and that their bodies may continue to be hallowed temples of the Holy Ghost. O God, lover of pure souls, let my children belong to the number of Thy favorites; let the blessing and the happiness and prosperity which, according to Thy gracious dispositions, accompany holy purity come upon my children. Amen.

Holy Virgin Mary, most chaste mother and intercessor of pure souls; St. Joseph, most chaste spouse of the Holy Virgin, St. Aloysius, angel in the flesh; and all ye holy virgins and children, and all ye Saints in heaven, assist me with your powerful intercession, so that the Lord, who has given you the grace of unimpaired innocence and chastity, may also bestow this same great gift upon my children. Amen.

*Prayer to obtain for the Children a True and Genuine Love of their Neighbor.**

O God of charity! who lovest all men as Thy children, and hast enjoined upon us all so sacredly that we too should sincerely love one another, inspire my children with this spirit of charity. Destroy in them all self-

---

* How great is the absence of Christian charity in every-day life, although it is one of the most fundamental virtues of a Christian! How necessary for mothers to cultivate this virtue in their children, and encourage them first of all in the practice of it to their sisters and brothers, and to ask frequently of God the gift of Christian charity for them!

interest and self-love; enlarge their hearts, that for Thy sake they may also love all men. Grant that they may live in peace and concord with one another in order that, after the exercise of love in the family has become, as it were, their second nature, they may, when occasion offers, extend this love to all men. Through Jesus Christ, our Lord. Amen.

Prayer to obtain for the Children the Love of Truth.

O God of Truth! who hatest all falsehood, guard my children from the shameful and pernicious vice of lying; for it renders them hateful in Thy sight. Teach them to love truth, and inspire them with horror of all kinds of falsehood. Amen.

Prayer to be said for the Children when frequenting School.

O God, Father of light! look graciously down upon my children, who are now attending school. What a precious occasion for the development of mind and heart, and for the acquirement of necessary and useful knowledge, they are now enjoying! Grant that they may use it faithfully and zealously. Keep within bounds their youthful levity and fickleness, and urge them to earnest diligence. Assist them that they may understand and remember well whatever they are taught. Especially visit them with Thy heavenly light, that they may understand well the teachings of our holy religion; open their young and tender hearts, that they may receive the Christian truths with beneficial results. Guard them from the bad influence of wicked children, and lead them into the company of those who may have a salutary influence upon them. Give Thy blessing to the priests, the teachers, and to all who work for my children, that their influence may be salutary and effective. Reward them for what they do. Grant that the school may be a preparation for the eternal happiness of my children in heaven. Amen.

*Prayer to be said for a Child when preparing for its First Confession.**

Most holy and merciful God! I recommend to Thee my child, which is now preparing for its first confession. It is from

* According to the doctrine of holy Church, the grace of true contrition and the willingness to do penance is a

Thee that true sorrow cometh; without Thy grace no one can be truly sorry for his sins or obtain Thy pardon. Send an abundance of Thy grace into the heart of my child, in order that it may overcome the levity of youth and prepare with earnestness, be truly sorry for its sins, confess them sincerely, and obtain pardon in the holy sacrament of penance. Grant that my child may, with the assistance of the father confessor and through this holy exercise, experience a salutary influence and be induced to give itself for the future with increased fidelity to the practice of a truly Christian life. Amen.

O holy angels, accompany my child and help him to make a good confession. Amen.

Prayer to be said for the Child when preparing for First Communion.

Divine Saviour, the time is drawing near when my child will enjoy for the first time the incomparable grace of receiving Thee in holy communion. Immeasurable is Thy

fruit of the holy sacrifice of the Mass. The Christian mother should, therefore, assist at holy Mass with the intention of obtaining for her children the grace to make a good confession. She should especially ask for them the grace of true contrition.

love for my child; therefore Thou wilt come to take up Thy abode in its soul, to unite it intimately and wholly to Thee, to enrich it with Thy most precious graces and lead it to the enjoyment of the greatest happiness. O Jesus, who can measure Thy goodness and condescension! Be Thou praised for all eternity! Oh, that my child may understand the greatness of the favor and the happiness Thou art preparing for it! Enlighten it and lead it to a knowledge of Thee; assist it to prepare well and receive worthily this great sacrament. Visit Thy servant who is preparing my child, that through Thy grace his instructions may have the salutary effect of making my child understand the Christian truths, and his words and direction lead it to the practice of a truly Christian life. O Jesus, grant that my child may use this time of preparation in such a profitable manner that it may approach the holy table with the proper dispositions, and receive Thee, my divine Lord, worthily into its soul. Amen.

Prayer that God may dispose for the best the Temporal Affairs of the Child.

All things, O God! rest in thy hands. "Thy power reacheth from one end of the world to the other, and disposeth all things well." Thou ordainest all things, that they may serve to lead men to true sanctity of life, for which Thou hast created them; and Thou hast created them for this end, that they may glorify Thy holy name and be truly happy for time and eternity. Thou, God of all knowledge, knowest the way in which my children will arrive most surely at this true happiness. Therefore, I beseech Thee, lead them graciously in this way. May Thy holy will be done in all things in their regard; for obedience to Thy will is their salvation. Do not permit me to be so blinded by selfish, earthly motives that I may lead them into paths which, though good in appearance, may end at last in their perdition. Guard them, that they may not go astray, deceived by the levity of youth. O great, infinitely wise, infinitely merciful, and powerful Father of my children! I implore Thee, be Thou Thyself their guide.

I implore Thee especially so to dispose

the ways of my children by Thy wisdom and power that each one may enter that state of life to which Thou hast called them. In their vocation Thine own free gift is to be found their full happiness on earth. Therefore, do not permit my children to be so overcome by sin and wicked inclinations as to be disobedient to Thy call. Give them and preserve in them a lively faith; confirm them in Thy holy fear and in true piety; for thus they will by Thy grace recognize in due time their vocation; thus they will give themselves up to it unhesitatingly, and Thou wilt be with them. Hear me, O my God, I implore Thee, and grant my petition. Through Jesus Christ. Amen.

*Prayer to be said for Children who are addicted to Certain Faults.**

Almighty God! rich in graces Thou who directest the hearts of men like rivers of

---

* It happens quite often that certain faults make their appearance in children, especially in those who are grown, which parents, notwithstanding their care and attention, cannot succeed in eradicating. In regard to the older children, the mother herself may be the remote cause of their faults, inasmuch as she did not sooner make an earnest effort to correct them. What remains for the mother to do? Should she lose courage? By no means!

water, graciously listen to my supplication in behalf of my son—[my daughter]. Thou knowest how much the sad condition of his [her] soul fills my heart with sorrow and anxiety. All my endeavors in his [her] regard prove fruitless. What remains for me but to take refuge in Thee? Thou art, O God, "powerful to bestow every grace in abundance," and to move with Thy grace the most hardened hearts. How often hast Thou brought back the most obstinate sinners! How often hast Thou listened to the prayers of pious mothers, and for their sake granted to their children the grace of true conversion! Therefore, despise not my prayer, though I confess it is not worthy of being heard. I have sinned before Thee, and I myself may partly be the cause of my son's

On the contrary, she should try every means in her power to correct them of the faults, wherein lies the danger of their ruin. And should all other efforts prove unsuccessful, one yet remains ; it is earnest, suppliant, persevering prayer. Would to God that all mothers, following the example of St. Monica, would make the right use of this means! How many a child whose faults are increasing, how many a son or daughter hastening to destruction, would receive through a mother's prayer sufficient grace to correct their faults and avert thus a great danger of being lost!

[daughter's] faults and errors. But, O merciful God! pardon me, since I am truly sorry for my sins. Let mercy take the place of justice. Through Thy infinite mercy, through the merits of Thy divine Son, my Saviour, through the intercession of the most blessed Virgin Mary, of St. Monica, and of all the Saints in heaven, I entreat Thee, visit my son [my daughter] with Thy grace, that he [she] may see his [her] faults, be heartily sorry for them, and, henceforward walking in all things according to Thy holy will and divine pleasure, obtain salvation.

O Mary, Mother of Mercy, refuge of sinners, St. Monica, who hast been especially victorious in thy prayers for thy Son, and all Ye Saints in heaven, assist me in my supplication with your mighty intercession, that it may be granted! Amen.

Prayer to obtain for Children the Seven Gifts of the Holy Ghost.

O Spirit of Holiness! make Thine abode with my children, in order that God's holy grace and the salvation of their souls may be always regarded by them as more valuable than all things else, and that they may always keep the eye of their souls directed towards heaven.

O Holy Ghost! give to my children the gift of Understanding, that they may comprehend more and more the teachings of our holy religion and grow zealous, whilst by listening to the Word of God and by pious reading they advance in the knowledge of Christian truth.

O Holy Ghost! give to my children the gift of Knowledge, that they may lay up an ever-increasing store of useful, salutary knowledge for their own and their neighbor's salvation.

O Holy Ghost! give to my children the gift of Counsel, that they may always see in the light of Thy grace what is according to God's holy will and useful for their salvation.

O Holy Ghost! give to my children the gift of Fortitude, that strengthened thereby they may not yield to difficulties in the practice of virtue, nor be discouraged by impediments, but persevere courageously and generously on the road to heaven. Amen.

O Holy Ghost! give to my children the gift of Piety; fill their hearts wholly with divine love, so that they may always be zealous in all good works, and be solely intent upon fulfilling in all things God's holy will.

O Holy Ghost! give to my children the gift of the Fear of God, in order that, recognizing sin as the greatest and only evil, they may abhor it and fear above everything else to become victims of God's divine justice. Amen.

THE HOLY WAY OF THE CROSS TO BE MADE BY CHRISTIAN MOTHERS FOR THE BENEFIT OF THEIR CHILDREN.

DIVINE SAVIOUR! Thou didst reveal to us all the riches of the love of Thy Sacred Heart during those hallowed hours of Thy bitter Passion and Death. Without compassion for Thyself Thou didst enter upon the way of suffering whilst Thy human nature was filled with horror and recoiled against it. But the love for Thy Father and for men triumphed over the aversion of Thy human nature, and the desire to obtain our salvation prevailed upon Thee to deliver Thyself up to all the disgrace, afflictions, and torments that were awaiting Thee, even to death on the Cross. Thus Thy sufferings and Thy death have become for us the fountain of salvation and of eternal life. Through Thee we receive pardon of our sins; through Thee we obtain every grace needed to secure the possession of heaven and of that happiness which will never again be lost. Eternal love, praise, and thanksgiving be to Thee! In spirit I will follow on the way of Thy bitter passion, to honor it and to ask, through its merits, for my children those graces by which they may be freed from all their sins and be enabled to know Thy charity, to love Thee with their whole hearts, and, through the faithful fulfilment of Thy commandments, to become partakers of the salvation which Thou hast obtained for them. My sins render me unworthy to appear in Thy presence, or to obtain what I ask. O Lord! pardon me! I am truly sorry for my sins. Assist me with Thy grace, that this devotion may please Thee. May the indulgences to be gained by this devotion be granted for my own and my children's benefit. Amen.

Hail Mary, Mother of Sorrows, accompany

me, and help my children with Thy powerful intercession. Amen.

I. STATION.—*Jesus is condemned to death.*
V *We adore Thee, O Lord Jesus Christ, and bless Thy holy name.*
R. *Because by Thy holy Cross Thou hast redeemed the world.**

Contemplate Jesus, meekly standing before the judge. His head crowned with thorns; His whole body torn with cruel scourges; exhausted unto death by His suffering in the garden, and by the treatment which He had already endured at the houses of Caiphas, Pilate, and Herod, but especially by what He suffered in His soul. Now the sentence of death is pronounced upon Him, the Most Holy; He is willing to die as a malefactor, in order to avert from us the sentence of eternal damnation. Pray to Him that because of this unjust, cruel sentence He may deliver Thy children from eternal death.

PRAYER.—O Jesus! it was for us that Thou didst permit that most unjust sentence to be pronounced upon Thee. Through it, I

* To be repeated at each Station.

entreat Thee, avert from my children and myself the sentence of eternal damnation.

Our Father. Hail Mary. Glory be to the Father.

V. Crucified Lord Jesus.

R. Have mercy on us.

II. STATION.—*Jesus receives the Cross.*

Contemplate how Jesus voluntarily takes the heavy Cross upon His shoulders, although exhausted, and fully aware of the suffering He will have to endure; that He must even die upon it, yet He embraces it. But through His suffering and death He will obtain our salvation. Therefore He willingly submits. Entreat Him to grant to your children the grace always to take willingly upon themselves His yoke, and to lead a truly Christian life.

PRAYER.—O Jesus, Thou who didst willingly take upon Thyself the heavy burden of the Cross, bless through Thy grace the endeavors of the priest and teachers, as well as my own, in behalf of my children, that they may be animated with a spirit pleasing to God, lead truly Christian lives, and be ever ready to take upon themselves Thy yoke and carry it perseveringly. Amen.

III. STATION.—*Jesus falls the first time under the weight of the Cross.*

The Cross is too heavy for Jesus. His strength fails Him. Through love for us, He is willing to carry it until He falls under its weight. Entreat Him to guard your children from dangers during their youth, and to support them that they may not fall.

PRAYER.—O Jesus, Thou who for our sins didst bear the heavy burden of the Cross until Thou didst fall under its weight, through the merits of this Thy fall I entreat Thee to protect my children amidst the manifold dangers of youth, that they may not fall into sin. O Lord, protect them always and lead them happily to their eternal destination. Amen.

IV. STATION. — *Jesus meets His holy Mother.*

Contemplate Jesus after having taken up again the Cross. He is met by His holy Mother. How the sight of Him must have pierced that Mother's heart! Who can understand her affliction? Ah, what a grief for Jesus, to see His holy Mother the victim of so great a sorrow! He loves her so intensely. Entreat our Lord that, through the compassion which filled His heart for His afflicted Mother. He may inspire children with a genuine love for their parents, and help them to discharge faithfully their duties.

PRAYER.—Divine Saviour, best and most loving of Sons, by the charitable compassion which Thou didst feel for Thy most afflicted Mother, grant to my children the grace to fulfil faithfully the duties of filial love and obedience to their parents, that the blessing of the fourth commandment and Thy good pleasure may abound in them. Amen.

V. STATION.—*Simon of Cyrene helps Jesus to carry the Cross.*

Contemplate Jesus as He staggers under the weight of the Cross. He is at every moment in danger of falling again. Ah, he is weary and exhausted, He is unable to proceed! The Cross is too heavy; Simon of Cyrene is compelled to help Him to carry it. Through the ignominy and pain experienced by Jesus in carrying the Cross, entreat Him to give your children the grace to bear courageously the troubles and difficulties of a Christian life, and to persevere in carrying their cross cheerfully to the end.

PRAYER.—O Jesus! who didst bear for us

the heavy burden of the Cross, excite in the hearts of my children the desire of imitating Thee; inspire them with holy courage to undergo willingly all the difficulties and troubles of a pious life, and give them strength to persevere. Amen.

VI. STATION.—*Jesus presents to Veronica the Image of His Sacred Countenance.*

Contemplate the pitiful sight of your Lord. His divine countenance, disfigured by blows, is covered with blood oozing from the wounds made by the crown of thorns. Veronica, the noble-hearted woman who offers Him a cloth, that He may wipe His sacred face, receives it back from Him with the impression of His holy countenance upon it. Entreat the Lord that He may imprint upon your children's hearts the memory of His passion, and enkindle in them a sincere devotion to it.

PRAYER.—O Jesus! Thou hast always enriched Thy elect with a tender devotion to Thy bitter passion, and through it hast moved them to the practice of all virtues; grant this favor also to my children; teach them to venerate Thee tenderly in Thy sufferings! Inflame their tender hearts more and more with the fire of Thy holy love, and with zeal for all that is good and pleasing to Thee. Amen.

VII. STATION.—*Jesus falls a second time.*

Contemplate how pitifully our Lord lies under the Cross on the ground. The weight of our sins has overpowered Him. Oh, what a great evil sin is, if God must punish it thus in His only begotten Son! Entreat the Lord to graciously guard your children from the guilt of mortal sin.

PRAYER.—O Jesus! falling again under the heavy burden of our sins, have mercy on my children. Ah, how much they are exposed to the danger of falling into mortal sin, surrounded as they are by so many temptations! Therefore I beseech Thee, through the merits of Thy fall under the Cross, guard them against the greatest of all misfortunes, that of losing Thee by sin! Do not permit them ever to lose Thy grace and friendship. Preserve them by the power of Thy holy name. Amen.

VIII. STATION.—*Jesus is lamented over by the women of Jerusalem.*

Contemplate how Jesus, when forced to take the Cross once more upon His shoulders, now scarcely able to proceed, totters under its weight. Pious women are moved to tears of compassion by this pitiful sight. Jesus in the midst of His sufferings looks upon them with grateful love. Entreat Him that He may inspire the hearts of your children with love and compassion for their suffering neighbor.

PRAYER.—Suffering Saviour, who in the midst of Thy sufferings didst look with gracious love upon those compassionate women, through the sad spectacle which moved these pious women to tears, I entreat Thee to animate the hearts of my children with the spirit of charity which, according to Thy holy will, is to be the mark by which those who belong to Thee are to be recognized. Grant that they may have compassion for their suffering brethren and be always ready to assist them cheerfully by word, deed, and prayer. Grant that they may love Thee in all who belong to Thee. Amen.

IX. STATION.—*Jesus falls the third time under the Cross.*

Contemplate how Jesus, having now arrived near the place where He was to be crucified, sinks totally exhausted under the heavy weight of the Cross. There, prostrate upon the ground, He suffers an agony of pains and sorrow. He has sacrificed all His strength in the work of our salvation. Entreat Him, through the merits of these exertions, to give to your children the grace of fervor in His service.

PRAYER.—O Jesus! Thou hast exhausted all Thy strength so far as even to sink under the heavy burden of Thy sufferings, in order to fulfil the work of our salvation; I entreat Thee, through the merits of this Thy third fall, to protect my children against the shame and evil of lukewarmness and indolence in Thy holy service. Incite them by Thy grace to a holy fervor, that they may employ all their strength of body and soul in the all-important work of honoring God and their salvation. Amen.

X. STATION.—*Jesus is stripped of His garments.*

They have at last arrived at the place of crucifixion. Without the least sense of pity the executioners cruelly tear the garments from His sacred body. The wounds are laid open and bleed once more; the crown of thorns, beaten and shattered, renews its cruel pains. Covered with bleeding wounds, Jesus stands exposed to the gaze of the multitude. Oh, most shocking sight! Offer to God all these pains. Ask for your children, through them, that He may keep afar the shame, the misfortune, and ruin of impurity.

PRAYER.—O my Saviour! Thou didst endure for my sake this confusion and pain; deeply moved with compassion, I adore Thy mercy and charity, and ask, through the greatness of Thy sufferings, one of the most precious gifts for my children. Yes, O Lord, through Thy nakedness, so extremely painful to Thee, I implore Thee take my children under the protection of Thy grace, that they may be guarded and removed far from the shame and the misfortune of impurity; fill their hearts with the grace of holy chastity, that they may love it and preserve it uninjured, and become participators in the fulness of its blessings. Amen.

XI. STATION.—*Jesus is nailed to the Cross.*
Contemplate how cruelly the executioners treat our Lord. He lays Himself upon the Cross, and stretches forth His sacred hands and feet to be pierced with nails and fastened to the Cross. Listen to the sound of

the hammers; the utmost intensity of pain is felt in every limb. There He lies, fastened to the tree of the Cross! Entreat Him, through the sufferings He endured in being nailed to the Cross, that the evil inclinations of nature may die in your children, especially that inordinate sensuality which is the cause of so many sins. Amen.

XII. STATION.—*Jesus dies upon the Cross.*
Contemplate Thy divine Saviour hanging on the Cross, all covered with wounds. His sacred blood is oozing from every part of His body. Rejected and despised by men, abandoned by His heavenly Father, who can fully estimate His sufferings? This is the high price wherewith He has bought our souls and saved them from eternal damnation. Oh, how precious are our souls! Recommend to the Lord the souls of your children.

PRAYER.—O Jesus! not with corruptible things, such as gold and silver, were our souls purchased, but with Thy precious blood, with Thy bitter sufferings and the sacrifice of Thy precious life. The souls of my children are precious in Thy sight. O Lord, assist me to protect them and lead them to salvation. Let not the high price which Thou hast paid for them be lost. Lead them to eternal life. Amen.

XIII. STATION.—*The sacred body of Jesus is laid in the arms of His holy Mother.*

Contemplate the sacred body after Jesus had expired on the Cross, covered with wounds from the crown of His head to the sole of His feet. The divine mother receives into her arms her lifeless Son. With what thankfulness and love would you look upon the dead body of a friend who, whilst following the impulse of his love, to save you and your children from the impending danger of death, had himself fallen a victim thereto? Jesus is this good friend. Entreat Him to give you and your children the grace to be always truly thankful and to return love for love.

PRAYER.—O Jesus! infinitely generous and noble friend, Thou hast given Thyself up, even unto death on the Cross, for me and for my children, to save us from eternal death. Do not allow us to become lukewarm and ungrateful, to forget such love. Grant that we may love Thee in return with our whole hearts, adhere to Thee always with invincible fidelity, and praise Thee forever in heaven. Amen.

XIV. STATION.—*The body of Jesus is laid in the Sepulchre.*

Contemplate the body of your Lord lying in the sepulchre. The great work which was imposed upon Him by His Father has been accomplished. He has fulfilled perfectly His Father's will. Now the glory of the Resurrection, the majestic joys of heaven, are approaching. Entreat the Lord to give to your children the grace to finish well their course, so that they, too, may have a glorious resurrection and enjoy the happiness of heaven.

PRAYER.—Divine Saviour! through Thy sacred rest in the sepulchre, I entreat Thee to lead my children through the manifold dangers and temptations of this life to a happy death, to a glorious resurrection, and to eternal life. Amen.

Concluding Prayer.

O most holy Trinity! let my devotion be pleasing to Thee! Graciously grant the petitions I have just offered in behalf of my children. Watch over them now and forever! O Almighty, all-merciful God! let none of them be lost! Grant that they may with me enter heaven. Amen.

At the end, the *Our Father*, the *Hail Mary*, and the *Glory be to the Father* may be said for the intention of the Sovereign Pontiff.

THE ROSARY OF THE CHRISTIAN MOTHER.

[The words are to be added after the Sacred Name in the Hail Mary of each decade of the Rosary.]

I. For Herself.

1. Who will grant me the grace of giving good example to my children.
2. Who will give me wisdom for the salutary education of my children.
3. Who will guard me against untimely indulgence and against all kinds of irritating words and actions.
4. Who will give me zeal and perseverance in the proper education of my children.
5. Who will bless my labors for the education of my children.

II. For her Children.

1. Who will guard my children in all dangers of body and soul.

2. Who will deliver my children from their evil inclinations.*

3. Who will give to my children and increase in them the spirit of the fear of God and of piety.†

4. Who will bestow upon my children the blessing of the fourth commandment.‡

---

* Or according to circumstances, instead of "their evil inclinations" the following may be inserted. "from their inclination to tell lies, to look for delicacies; from their stubbornness and disobedience; from their idleness, indolence, want of desire to acquire useful knowledge; from their wantonness and dissoluteness; from their quarrelsomeness; from their levity, want of consideration; from impurity; from their desire for sensual pleasures; from their indifference with regard to God and religion," etc.

† According to circumstances, instead of "the spirit of the fear of God and piety" the following may be inserted: "the gift of faith; the gift of divine love; the gift of zeal in prayer and divine service; the virtues of humility and modesty; the grace of temperance; the gift of true love for their neighbor; the grace of compassion for the poor."

‡ That is to say, "Who will graciously incite in my children a great desire to fulfil faithfully their duties towards their parents, in order that they may become partakers of the blessing promised to those who keep the fourth com-

5. Who will preserve my children from the misfortune of mortal sin.*

mandment." Duties towards parents, it is clear, are of all duties the most important for children; in the fulfilment of them is contained all that constitutes their true happiness. The more perfectly they fulfil the duties of esteeming, loving, and obeying their parents, the more pleasing they will be in the sight of God, and the better founded will be the expectation that in the other relations of life they will prove worthy of confidence. What more precious grace could a mother ask for her children than the grace to keep faithfully the fourth commandment?

* By way of change, or for other reasons, *e.g.*, to obtain for them the grace to prepare well for the confession they are about to make, the following may be inserted : " Who will give my son [daughter] the grace of true contrition, a good confession, or the grace to prepare themselves well for holy communion. Who will give to my son [daughter] a great desire to study his [her] holy religion, and light to understand it well. Who will give to my son [daughter] the grace to prepare well for his [her] first communion." During the days preceding the first communion the following may be said : " Who will prepare with Thy grace the heart of my child, that it may become a worthy dwelling for Thy divine majesty." When a son or daughter leaves home : " Who will take my son under His special protection, and preserve his soul untarnished in His grace." With regard to the choice of a state of life : " Who will lead my son [daughter], by the light of divine grace, to the knowledge of his [her] true vocation," etc.

PRAYER OF THE MOTHER WHEN PREPARING TO GO TO CONFESSION.*

Preparatory Prayer.

Alas! I have hitherto been remiss in the conscientious and faithful discharge of the most sacred duties which I owe to my children. O Lord, grant that I may become fully aware of the faults and errors I have committed, so that I may be truly sorry for them and obtain pardon. I wish this holy confession to enkindle within me new zeal and fervor, so that I may be enabled henceforward to regard my duties as holy, and to fulfil them with all possible conscientiousness and fidelity. Through Jesus Christ, our Lord. Amen.

Prayer to be added to the Act of Contrition.

O my God! my guilt is rendered greater because I have neglected my duties towards the children whom Thou hast entrusted to my care. Thou requirest of me that I should lead a life pleasing to Thee, in order that I may be able to rear my children in Thy holy

---

* To be added to the usual prayers for confession, or inserted between them.

fear and love. It is necessary that I should give them good example. But, alas! how deficient I have been in this! Because of my coldness toward Thee, because of my negligence in Thy holy service, because of my sins, my teachings have remained fruitless and without Thy blessing. How often have they not seen in me sins and imperfections injurious to the souls of my children! They have also remained poor in grace, because I have prayed but little and negligently for them. O my God! how can I appear before Thee at the last judgment, where I shall learn that I have given only scandal and occasions of sin to those whom Thou has confided to me to instruct and lead them in the paths of virtue! Woe to me if those whom I am called to lead to heaven should perish through my fault!

And how confounded must I stand before Thee! How dear are my children to Thee; how much dost Thou love them! What great things hast Thou done for them! Thou hast offered up for them Thy beloved Son, and He has not hesitated to undergo on their account the greatest possible sufferings, and even to die for them on the Cross!

For their eternal welfare the same divine Son has left in His holy Church all treasures of salvation and grace; yes, He is even ready to give Himself to my children in holy communion, that he may lead them to the port of salvation. And I have esteemed these souls so little, who are so precious in Thy sight and so much loved by Thee; I have neglected them, even added my share to bring about their ruin. Oh, ungrateful creature that I am! How much have I offended, how deeply have I afflicted Thy divine and fatherly heart! Out of Thy love for me Thou hast called me to be a mother. What a precious occasion does not this offer to me to make myself pleasing in Thy sight! Through the fulfilment of my duties toward my children I hope to receive an abundance of merits, and be rewarded by participating for all eternity in the happiness which Thou dost enjoy in the midst of Thy children. But alas! I have corresponded very imperfectly with the intentions of Thy fatherly goodness!

O my God! I have sinned; but I am sincerely sorry for my sins, and with the help of Thy grace I resolve to amend my life.

My duties shall henceforward be sacred to me. I shall spare no pains to fulfil them most faithfully. And in order to do this I will try to avoid every fault and set a good example to my children. Look upon Thy divine Son, my Saviour, and for His sake forgive me my sins! Assist me with Thy grace, that I may henceforward keep faithfully my resolutions. Amen.

Additional Prayer after Confession.

Heartily do I rejoice, O my God, that I am permitted to look upon Thee again as my loving Father; for the sins which I have committed as a mother Thou hast now graciously forgiven me. I renew, therefore, my promises of amendment before Thee. As it is one of my most sacred duties, I shall endeavor now most earnestly to do Thy holy will as a mother, and to be to my children a truly Christian mother. To this end I will be the more zealous to exercise myself in the true fear of Thy majesty and piety. I will be most careful to avoid in my words and actions whatever can be displeasing to Thee, and give my children in all things a good example. I will diligently strive to induce them to correct their faults and to practice all kinds of virtue. I will never cease to pray for them.

O God, Thou hast given me again a good will. Help me also to accomplish what I have resolved to do. Without thy grace I can do nothing. Assist me, then! Make me by the virtue of Thy grace always more like to those holy mothers who have educated their children to become Saints. Amen.

(Say here, as much as time will allow, some of the prayers on page 175, etc.)

PRAYER AT HOLY COMMUNION.*

O divine Saviour! Thou hast in this Thy holy mystery of love left us a fountain of the richest graces. From it we derive strength to be worthy of our Christian vocation, and to arrive at last at the eternal happiness of true children of God. How much do I also stand in need of this rich source of grace, to fulfil as I should all the duties of a Christian mother! Therefore I now come to Thee, O Jesus! Thou friend of children. Do Thou also draw nigh to me. Come into

* To be added to the Preparatory Prayer.

my heart and enrich me with Thy graces, that I may henceforward be better able to educate the children whom Thou hast confided to me, and whom Thou lovest so much, wholly according to Thy holy will and desire. Without the light and strength of Thy grace I cannot do it. Come then to my assistance, O Lord! strengthen me, that I may also persevere in the faithful discharge of my duties to the end. Renew by this holy Communion in me all those graces which Thou hast offered to me in the sacrament of matrimony. Mould my heart anew according to the pattern of a Christian mother's heart, so that my greatest care may be the true welfare of my children, and that I may do willingly whatever may be necessary or useful for them. Amen.

Additional Prayer to be said after Communion.

O Jesus! who art now truly present in my soul and most intimately united to me, Thou hast come to sanctify my heart by Thy holy presence, and to unite me yet more intimately with Thee through love. Thou art come to nourish me with Thy grace, and to enable me to lead a life pleasing to Thee.

Thou art come to me, divine Friend of children, also for the sake of my children. They also are objects of Thy parental concern. Thou hast the most loving desire that they may grow up faithful members of Thy holy Church and obtain their eternal salvation. It is Thy loving intention to enable me through this holy Communion to lead as a mother Thy beloved children to this happy end. Make me, through the virtue of Thy powerful grace, a truly good mother; enrich me with all truly maternal qualities and virtues; let Thy blessing rest upon whatever I may do for them. Oh, that it might have been granted me to live when Thou didst live among men! How should I have rejoiced to receive Thee as host like Martha and Mary! What would I have been more concerned about than to bring, as so many mothers did, also my children to Thee, that Thou mightest have blessed them! Shall I omit to do so to-day, when Thou, still more mercifully, becomest the host of my soul? No, divine Saviour, my heart impels me to lead in spirit all my children to Thee, and to recommend them to Thy divine goodness and grace. Take them, then, mercifully under Thy care! Without Thy help I can do nothing for their true welfare. Descend, therefore, in Thy goodness and be at my side in the work of educating my children! Guard them against sin! Fill their hearts with Thy holy love and with Thy Spirit, that they may always and in all things walk according to Thy holy will and example. Lead them to life eternal. Amen.

PRAYER OF A MOTHER FOR HER HUSBAND.*

O heavenly Father! Thou hast confided my children not to myself alone, but to my husband also. The true education of our children can only be accomplished, therefore, when we both are sincerely and earnestly intent upon fulfilling our duties toward them. Grant then, O Lord, also to my husband the grace to see and to understand

* Every good and Christian mother will also pray much and fervently for her husband, who is so intimately united to her. Especially will she do so when he is a victim to certain faults and bad habits, and whenever his soul is exposed to greater dangers. We have reference here, however, only to prayer to enable him to fulfil his duties as a father.

the sanctity and importance of his vocation as a father; urge him on to be zealous in fulfilling it perfectly. Oh, that above all he might go before our children with the example of a truly Christian life! O God, give him, therefore, Thy grace, that he may earnestly war against his faults and conquer them. May he not forget Thee in the midst of the distractions of daily life, and perish in the many dangers that surround him! Inspire him with lively sentiments of faith, hope, and charity; give him zeal for prayer and divine service, and for all the exercises of a Catholic Christian. Make him a truly good father toward his children. Amen.

PRAYER TO OBTAIN THE VIRTUE OF CHASTITY CONFORMABLE TO A MOTHER'S VOCATION.

O God! Thou lover of pure souls; Thou "from whom every perfect gift proceedeth," I

---

* This prayer is inserted with good reason among the prayers of a Christian mother, for if the successful education of children depends especially upon the piety of the mother, it is only in a chaste heart that such true piety may be expected to flourish. It is, therefore, God's holy will that married people also should live a chaste life. Remember here the words of the Angel Raphael to the

too come to Thee, and entreat Thee with my whole heart for the grace and gift of chastity, which belongs to my state of life; for I know that I cannot be chaste except Thou givest it. Oh, grant then this great grace to me! How precious in Thy sight is the chaste life of married people who are pure in heart! Upon them Thy eye rests with delight. They experience the blessing of Thy

younger Tobias: "For they who in such manner receive matrimony as to shut out God from themselves and from their mind, and to give themselves to their lust, as the horse and mule, which have not understanding, over them the devil hath power." (Tobias vi. 17.) This has reference to the seven husbands of Sarah, who all died suddenly in the night following the marriage. "I have heard" said Tobias (vi. 14) "that a devil killed them," and the angel confirmed it. "But thou," continued the angel, "take the Virgin with the fear of the Lord, moved rather for love of children than for lust." And Tobias spoke thus to Sarah, his wife: "We are the children of saints, and we must not be joined together like heathens, that know not God." But in order that Christian married people may come together as becomes children of Saints, that is to say Christians, and live in chastity belonging to their state of life, they stand in need of a particular grace. "And as I knew that I could not otherwise be continent, except God gave it, . . . I went to the Lord and besought Him" for this grace "with my whole heart." (Wisd. viii. 21.) Behold here the reason for the above prayer. Would to God that it may be said often with the whole heart!

choicest gifts; from them descend prosperity, happiness, and benediction upon their children. Oh, how beautiful is a chaste generation! Permit not that in my matrimonial life I should cast myself without restraint into the arms of sensual desires, like the horse and mule, who have no understanding. Do not permit me to cast under my feet holy shame, like the heathen, and thus, shutting Thee out of my heart, give the devil power over me. Let us come together as becometh the children of Saints, in the fear of God. Thou hast graciously given me a right to such a grace in the holy sacrament of matrimony, and Thou art ready to grant it to me if I ask for it as I should. O Lord, I entreat Thee, give it to me! It is in virtue of this grace that Thou dost at all times rear in Thy holy Church holy married people, who even in their married state lead a chaste life. Through it I too will be strong enough to bridle all inordinate desires; strengthened by it, I shall persevere faithfully within those limits which Thou hast fixed; enlightened and sanctified by it, I shall at all times, remembering the end of the matrimonial state, never allow to myself what is contrary to it. Thou by whom all things are possible, grant my petition! O holy Virgin Mary and Thou, her virgin spouse, Saint Joseph, and all ye holy fathers and mothers, pray for me. Amen.

PRAYER FOR A MOTHER WHEN WITH CHILD.

Almighty and all-merciful God, Creator and Preserver of all things, Thou who, according to the counsel of Thy wisdom and goodness, hast blessed my matrimonial union, how many reasons have I not to thank Thee for having held me worthy to coöperate in the fulfilment of Thy fatherly intentions, according to which Thou hast again given existence to a man, destined to glorify Thy holy name for time and eternity! Oh, that I may understand well my part now and perform it! Bless me, O my God, and bless my child, which I consecrate to Thee. Thou hast given it to me, and I give it back to Thee. Preserve this precious pledge under Thy fatherly protection, and assist me that I may avoid, as much as possible, whatever may have a pernicious influence on it. Guard me against bad inclinations and inordinate desires; against anger and indignation; against vanity, and against all that is sinful and displeasing in Thy sight. Inspire my heart with sentiments of true piety, and direct all my inclinations towards what is good and pleasing to Thee, so that already now the growing heart of my child may become inclined to what is truly good and perfect.

Be Thou, O God! my protection and defence, so that nothing hurtful may happen to me. O Father of men and of my children, mercifully bring Thy work in me to perfection, and grant that I may one day praise Thy holy name in the joy that a man has been born into the world. Through Jesus Christ. Amen.

PRAYER TO OBTAIN FOR A CHILD A VOCATION TO THE PRIESTHOOD.

Divine Saviour, how great is Thy desire for the salvation of men, and how great is Thy desire, therefore, for holy priests. To this end Thou dost admonish us to pray, saying: "Pray the Lord of the harvest, that

He may send workmen into His vineyard." O Jesus! would I be mindful of these words if I had no desire to see a son of mine a priest? I beseech Thee, therefore, O Lord, if it be not contrary to Thy holy decrees, inspire my son with a holy desire to work for the salvation of souls in the priesthood, and receive him among the number of Thy sacred ministers. "Thou directest the hearts of men like rivers of water." Thou didst change a persecuting Saul into an Apostle Paul. With thee all things are possible. Show then, O most powerful God, the power of Thy grace. Grant my petitions, O Lord. I know and confess that I am unworthy of so great a grace; but Thou art rich in graces, even unto those who are not worthy of them. Show Thyself merciful also unto me! If I may hope that my request shall be granted, I will endeavor to the utmost to lead my son, blessed and enriched with so sublime a vocation, into the acquirement of the true fear of God and piety, that he may become a worthy minister at the altar. Amen.

And ye, happy mothers in heaven, who have had the grace and consolation of giving worthy priests to holy Church, assist my unworthy prayer with the power of your intercession. Amen.

Prayer for a Son who already has a Vocation to the Priesthood.

O God! Thou who has deigned to bestow on me, so unworthy of it, the inestimable grace of being mother of a son called to the dignity of the priesthood, I entreat Thee with a thankful heart to preserve in him the good work Thou hast begun, and to bring it to perfection. Ah! how easily may this sublime vocation, through one's own fault, be lost! How great and numerous are the dangers of becoming unfaithful to it! I entreat Thee, therefore, O God! defend my son from these dangers; lead him so that he may without wavering persevere in the course beset by so many dangers, and keep constantly before his eyes the sublime end which he has in view. Visit him with the most precious blessing of Thy grace, that he may grow up and advance in true Christian piety. Assist him in his studies, in order that, well provided with science and understanding, he may be able to fulfil the duties of his vocation in a useful and profitable manner Give Thy grace and help also to me, that I may discharge the duties of my vocation to my son with the greatest fidelity and zeal, and omit nothing which may serve to give him an education corresponding to his high calling Bless then, all-merciful God, my endeavor with the power of Thy grace. Amen

Ye holy mothers who have educated holy priests, and who have, therefore, for all eternity a share in all the good they have done, and in their glory and happiness; and ye priests now reigning in heaven, pray for me, and obtain for me the grace so to educate my son that he may one day also become a worthy priest. Obtain also for my son the grace of perseverance, that he may triumph over the assaults of Satan, and be admitted among the number of the priests of the Most High. Amen.

LITANY FOR A CHRISTIAN MOTHER.

Lord, have mercy on me!
Christ, have mercy on me!
Lord, have mercy on me!
Christ, have mercy on me! Christ, graciously hear me!

God, the Father of heaven, have mercy on me!

Thou great Father, from whom all parental relation proceedeth,

O God, thou heavenly father of my children,

Thou who lovest my children more than I, their mother, can love them,

Thou who desirest that they may be forever happy with Thee,

Thou who hast delivered up Thy only Son for them also,

Thou who hast sent Thy angels to guard them,

Thou who hast confided them to my love and care,

Thou who requirest of me to keep and educate them for Thee,

Thou who art willing to assist and help me in this my work,

} Have mercy on me.

Thou who wilt call me one day to give a strict account of the manner in which I have fulfilled my duties to my children,

Thou who wilt reward in an unspeakable manner the faithful fulfilment of a mother's duties,

God the Son, Redeemer of the world,

Thou who hast become man for us,

O Jesus, who hast sanctified the tender age of childhood by having become a child Thyself,

O Jesus, Thou most lovely of children,

O Jesus, Thou most loving and faithful Son of Thy holy Mother and foster-father,

O Jesus, Thou friend of children,

Thou who hast pronounced condemnation upon all those who shall be guilty of scandal to their children,

Thou who regardest as done to Thyself whatsoever is done to children,

Thou who dost love my children, and hast offered Thyself up for them,

Thou who hast also for their sake enriched Thy holy Church with graces,

} Have mercy on me.

Thou who by the sacrament of penance hast consecrated and enabled me, with Thy grace, to fulfil the duties of a mother

Thou who hast prepared in Thy holy Church so many graces for this vocation,

God the Holy Ghost,

Thou who, through the workings of Thy grace in holy baptism, hast changed my children into children of God,

Thou by whose grace alone I can successfully fulfil my duties toward my children,

Thou by whose grace my children can become holy and remain so,

Thou Spirit of Wisdom and understanding,

Thou Spirit of Counsel and fortitude,

Thou Spirit of Piety and of the fear of God,

Thou Spirit of Knowledge and all graces,

Thou who hast often worked in children wonderful changes through the power of Thy grace.

Holy Trinity one God,

Have mercy on me.

Holy Mary,
Holy mother of God,
Mother of Christ,
Mother most pure,
Mother most chaste,
Mother most amiable,
Mother most admirable,
Thou who didst offer up Thy divine Son in the Temple,
Thou who didst flee with him into Egypt,
Thou who didst seek Him for three days with sorrow,
Thou who didst recommend the newly married people of Cana to Him,
Thou who didst see him suffer and die on the Cross,
Thou who didst hold Him in Thy arms after he had died
Thou who didst offer Him up willingly to the Father,
Thou who because of His resurrection and ascension into heaven wast filled with holy joy,
Thou who art now glorified with Him in heaven,
St. Joseph,

} Pray for me

Thou to whom God did confide what He esteemed most precious, His divine Son,

Thou who didst most carefully protect and cherish Thy divine foster-son,

Thou who didst have the blessing and consolation of working with Him so many years,

Thou who didst breathe out Thy last breath in His arms,

Ye holy guardian angels and friends of my children, who behold always the face of the heavenly Father,

Ye who are sent by God for the protection of my children,

Ye who, full of love for my children, are always intent upon guarding and defending them,

O blessed Anna, happy mother of the most blessed Virgin,

Thou who by a life of holy endurance, patience, and prayer didst obtain the honor of such a motherhood,

Thou whom God didst bless with a child of all that ever were born the richest in grace,

Thou who didst instruct Thy holy

daughter in the practice of all kinds of virtues and perfection,

Thou who didst go before her with the example of a most holy life,

Thou Patroness of Christian wives and mothers,

St. Joachim, Thou pious Consort of St. Anne,

O blessed Anne, Thou favored mother of Samuel,

Thou who didst obtain this child of benediction by Thy persevering prayer,

Thou who didst consecrate it to the service of the Tabernacle,

Holy mother of the Maccabees, thou martyr of the Old Testament,

Thou heroine and model of true motherly love,

Thou who didst deliver up Thy seven sons to death with unshaken fortitude for the law of the Lord,

St. Joachim, Thou father of the blessed Virgin Mary,

Ye holy mothers of the Apostles, who gave up your sons to our divine Saviour, and consecrated them to His service,

St. Felicitas, thou who, like the mother

} Pray for me.

of the Maccabees, didst deliver up Thy seven sons for Jesus unto death and martyrdom,

All ye holy mothers who have preferred to see your children die in the pains of martyrdom rather than to see them deny their faith,

St. Paula, Thou model of the love of a mother,

St. Monica, Thou who by Thy persevering prayers and entreaties didst win Thy son Augustine for God,

St. Elizabeth, Thou who didst educate Thy child with so great care,

All ye holy and chosen mothers,

Ye who through prayers and pious works have obtained the favor of motherhood,

Ye who have taken so great pains to educate, by word and example, the children whom the Lord confided to you, to true holiness of life,

Ye who, through the faithful fulfilment of your duties as mothers, have also arrived yourselves at sanctity, and at the possession of the highest happiness in heaven,

Pray for me.

All ye holy Angels,
All ye holy Patriarchs and Prophets,
All ye holy Apostles and Martyrs,
All ye holy Bishops, Priests and Confessors,
All ye holy Virgins and Widows,
All ye holy and innocent children,
} *Pray for me.*

Be merciful to me, spare me, O Lord!
Be merceiful to me, hear me, O Lord!
From all evil deliver me, O Lord!

From indifference to my vocation,
From the neglect of my duties as a mother,
From the disregard of the salvation of my children,
From imprudent love and indulgence,
From anger, and from a passionate manner of speaking and acting,
From all kinds of bad example,
From the spirit of uncleanness,
} *Deliver me, O Lord!*

Through the merits of Thy life, suffering, and death,
Through Thy love for children,
Through the great care which Thou didst manifest for children,
Through the great reward which Thou hast promised to those who for Thy sake receive children under their care,
} *I beseech Thee to hear me!*

Through the mercies of Thy divine Heart,

Through the intercession of Thy holy Mother,

Through the intercession of all mothers now happy in heaven.

I, a sinner, beseech Thee to hear me!

That Thou wouldst grant me the grace to understand fully the greatness and sublimity of my vocation,

That Thou wouldst assist me to arrive at a true knowledge of the importance of my duties towards my children,

That Thou wouldst give me, in the difficult work of education, understanding, judgment, and wisdom,

That Thou wouldst fill my heart with true love for my children,

That Thou wouldst give me fervor in prayer for my children,

That Thou wouldst bless my instructions and admonitions,

That Thou wouldst give me the grace to go before my children in all things, and always with the light of good example,

That Thou wouldst graciously take

my children under Thy Almighty protection,

That Thou wouldst guard them against all levity, and against the misfortune of mortal sin,

That Thou wouldst give them the grace of becoming well founded in the fear of God and piety, and of persevering therein,

That Thou wouldst increase in them Thy holy love,

That Thou wouldst preserve in them the treasure of unblemished innocence,

That Thou wouldst repel all the wicked attacks of hell,

That Thou wouldst guard them against all the bad influences of the world,

That Thou wouldst give Thy blessing to the endeavors of priests and teachers in their behalf,

That Thou wouldst preserve them in Thy grace,

That Thou wouldst lead them to eternal life,

} *I beseech Thee to hear me.*

Lamb of God, who takest away the sins of the world, spare me, O Lord.

Lamb of God, who takest away the sins of the world, graciously hear me, O Lord.

Lamb of God, who takest away the sins of the world, have mercy on me, O Lord.

Christ hear me! Christ graciously hear me!

Lord have mercy on me!
Christ have mercy on me!
Lord have mercy on me!
Our Father. Hail Mary.

Prayer.

O God, whose mercy is without measure, and whose goodness is without limit, I render thanks to Thee for the graces and favors which Thou hast so freely bestowed upon me and upon my children; and since Thou dost listen willingly to those who address Thee, I pray most earnestly that Thou wilt never abandon me and my children, but that Thou wouldst lead us to an eternal reward in heaven. Through Jesus Christ our Lord. Amen.

PRAYER TO THE SACRED HEART OF JESUS.

O most Sacred Heart of Jesus, Abode of the most perfect love, containing all perfection; worthy to be honored above all things by all hearts, I also offer unto Thee my sincere veneration; I love Thee with my whole heart, and I wish nothing else but to love Thee more and more, in order to consecrate to Thee all that I have and am.

O divine Heart, filled with so great and loving a care for men that Thou hast ordained and accomplished whatever was useful for their true welfare, and delivered Thyself up to ignominy and suffering, and even to death, for their sake, awake also in my heart similar sentiments of love, so that I too may be ready to offer sacrifices for the good of my neighbor, and to undergo troubles and difficulties. Inspire my heart especially with love for my children, similar to that which Thou hast for them, so that I may live wholly for them, and like Thee make every effort to lead them to eternal salvation.

To Thy loving Heart, O Jesus, I recommend my children. Encircle them, sanctuary of love, with Thy burning flames. Keep them so that no one may tear them from Thee. Thou knowest the dangers to which they are exposed, the enemies which threaten them. Have pity on them! According to the multitude of Thy mercies, hasten to their assistance. O most Sacred Heart of my Lord, wherein are contained all virtues and perfections, free my children from whatever is displeasing to Thee; destroy in them sin, and pardon them all the evil they have committed against Thee. Infuse into them out of Thy most Sacred Heart whatever is pleasing to Thee. Sanctify and take possession of them. Do in all things in their regard what is most pleasing to Thee, only preserve them in Thy holy love; cast them not away from Thee, I implore Thee. I call upon Thee, as upon my only hope, that Thou wouldst permit me and my children always to experience Thy mighty and powerful protection. Assist us all, each one according to his special need, above all at the hour of death; then call us to Thee, that our hearts may be forever united to Thy adorable Heart in love and eternal happiness. Amen.

PRAYERS TO BE SAID IN COMMON.

*Morning Prayer.**

O God, Heavenly Father! Thou hast permitted us again, after the rest of the night, to awake refreshed and in health. Thou hast given us this new day in order that we may glorify Thee in holiness of life. Assist us by the help of Thy grace. Thou hast also during the past night graciously preserved us from all evil, and for this we thank Thee heartily through Jesus Christ, our blessed Saviour. To-day we are resolved to live as good children; we will be on our guard not to do anything evil. We will beware of disobedience to our parents, of seeking after delicacies, of telling lies, and of quarrelling, fighting, wrangling, and disputing with other children and among ourselves. We will be

---

* In the instructive part we have recommended that the mother should make her children say their prayers in her presence, or in common with her, in the morning and evening. Here may be found prayers for this purpose. Christian mothers, gather your little ones around you, or, kneeling before a crucifix, pray with them. It will be of great advantage also to read these prayers slowly from time to time with the children, in order to explain them. This will cause them to pray with more devotion.

diligent and industrious in studying and working, and devout in our prayers, and often during the day we shall think of Thee, O God! Then we will be pleasing to Thee, our good Father, and Thou, our dear Saviour, wilt rejoice over us. Living thus, we will come one day to Thee in heaven. How great a happiness will we there enjoy with Thee! Yes, we will live as pious children. But, beloved Father, we cannot do so alone; help must come from Thee. Assist us; then we will keep our promise. Amen.

O Jesus, divine Saviour, how much Thou didst love children whilst upon earth! And now also Thou lovest ardently good children. When still a child, how good and pious Thou wast, how obedient to Thy parents, how devout in the temple, how diligent and industrious! Oh, help us, that we, too, may become good children like Thee. O Jesus, we love Thee with all our hearts. Grant that we may love Thee more and more. Amen.

Our Father, etc.

O Mary, Mother of our dear Saviour, Thou who art our Mother, pray to Thy beloved

Son for us, and obtain for us grace that we may become good children like Thy Child Jesus.

Hail Mary, etc.

O ye holy Guardian Angels, ye holy Patrons, whose names we bear; ye holy children, and all ye Saints, intercede for us! Intercede for us, that we may live so as to join at last your holy company in heaven. Amen.

O God and Father, we pray to Thee also for our dear parents. Oh, give also to them this day grace to do what is good; guard them against all evil; grant unto them what is profitable for them. We pray to Thee also for all those whom we love, and for all Christians; yes, for all men. Give to all, O God, what is good, and preserve them from all evil. Amen.

Evening Prayer.

O God, Heavenly Father, another day has passed away. Thou hast preserved us in health and strength. Meat and drink, whatsoever has caused us pleasure to-day, and all things which we have received, are Thy gift. O most bountiful and good Father, Thou hast also given us grace to do good and to avoid evil. O best and kindest Father, we thank Thee from the bottom of our hearts for all these things. But the best thanksgiving we can make is to do Thy will in all things; and this we resolve to do by Thy help.

But have we to-day been good and pious in every respect? [*A little pause for reflection.*] Alas! we have to-day again committed faults and sins, and we have offended Thee, dearest Father, and Thee, divine Saviour! We are heartily sorry for what we have done which has been displeasing to Thee. We promise Thee again that to-morrow we will be more careful. Give us Thy help, that we may keep our promise. Amen.

Now we lay ourselves down to rest. Guard us, Heavenly Father. Let Thy dear angels keep watch over us and preserve us from all evil.

Our Father.

O Holy Virgin Mary, help of Christians, we recommend ourselves also to Thy motherly care and protection. Abandon us not! Recommend us to Thy divine Son. Show that Thou art our Mother.

Hail Mary.

We pray to Thee, O God, Heavenly Father, also for all those whom we love; for our beloved parents, for our brothers and sisters, for our relations; we pray to Thee for all Christians, especially for those who are in need and danger, for the poor suffering souls in Purgatory, and for all men. Help them and conduct them all to Thyself in heaven. Amen.

When taking Holy Water before Retiring.

In the name of the Father, and of the Son, and of the Holy Ghost. Amen. In the name of Jesus, I lie down to sleep. O Jesus, Mary, Joseph, I recommend myself to you. Amen.

Before Meals.

O God, the food which we are now going to take is Thy gift. We thank Thee for it. Bless it and give us Thy grace, that we may be temperate in eating and receive it with a thankful heart. Through Jesus Christ, our Lord. Amen.

Our Father. Hail Mary.

After Meals.

We thank Thee, O God, for the gifts which we have just received. We thank Thee for all the good things which Thou dost so unceasingly give to us. Through the nourishment which we have just taken, Thou hast again refreshed us for Thy service. Help us by Thy grace always faithfully to conform to it. Through Jesus Christ our Lord. Amen.

Our Father. Hail Mary.

May the souls of the faithful departed, through the mercy of God, rest in peace. Amen.

Approbations to
THE CHRISTIAN FATHER.

ERIE, PA., Feb. 12, 1883.

It is much to be hoped, that not only every Catholic father, but every Catholic mother, as well as every Catholic son and daughter, will read and reread "THE CHRISTIAN FATHER." **What is said in it, and said so well,** on "Mixed Marriages," **entitles it to a place in every Catholic household.** T. MULLEN, *Bishop of Erie.*

BUFFALO, February 12, 1883.

The Catholic Public will, I think, thank you for the publication in English of "THE CHRISTIAN FATHER." Of the work itself I have fully enough expressed my opinion in the Introduction, but I may say that on reading Rev. F. Lambert's English translation, I seem to appreciate better than before the great value of the little book. **Had I the means I would make a present of "The Christian Father" to every Catholic father in the diocese.**
S. V. RYAN, *Bishop of Buffalo.*

ALTON, Feb. 14, 1883.

Please accept my sincere thanks for the complimentary copy of "THE CHRISTIAN FATHER." **Father Lambert has done a good work in bringing this book before our people in** English. Please send me a dozen copies.
✝ P. J. BALTES, *Bishop of Alton.*

INDIANAPOLIS, Ind., Feb. 9th, 1883.

.... Many thanks for the little book "THE CHRISTIAN FATHER." I have not had time to examine it thoroughly, but I see it is **a very useful work. It should be in the hand of every Christian Father,** as the "Christian Mother" should be carefully read by every mother who loves her children.
✝ F. S. CHATARD, *Bishop of Vincennes.*

BENZIGER BROTHERS, New York, Cincinnati, and St. Louis.

Approbations to
A SURE WAY TO A HAPPY MARRIAGE.

Paper, 30 cents; maroquette, rich, full gilt side, 40 cents; cloth, red edges, 60 cents.

"* * * A Sure Way to a Happy Marriage," I would like to see in the hands of all who have entered or propose to enter the holy state of wedlock." *Pastoral* of the Right Rev. Bishop of Buffalo. Feb. 20, 1882.

"* * * * Most useful to parents and young people. I wish it a wide circulation."
✠ CHAS. J. SEGHERS, *Archbishop of Oregon.*

"A most useful course of instructions, and should be duly read by all interested in Christian guidance for the Sacrament of Matrimony.
✠ THOMAS A. BECKER, *Bishop of Wilmington.*

"* * * * A most useful contribution to Catholic literature; while the question it deals with is one that ought to secure it a wide circulation among all classes and creeds."
✠ T. MULLEN, *Bishop of Erie.*

"* * * * I cheerfully and heartily commend it. * * Its instructions are practical, solid, and as useful as they are needed. ✠ S. V. RYAN, *Bishop of Buffalo.*

"* * * * ought to be well received by the public."
✠ EDGAR P. WADHAMS, *Bishop of Ogdensburg.*

"* * * * A book well suited to our times. * * We most sincerely wish for it a wide circulation among our young people." ✠ W. H. GROSS, *Bishop of Savannah.*

"* * * * We recommend it most highly to those for whom it is written." ✠ RUPERT SEIDENBUSH, O.S.B., *Vicar Apostolic of Northern Minnesota.*

"* * * * If its counsels and instructions be followed it will guide those who contemplate entering into this state, and will ensure happiness to those who are already united by this sacred bond." ✠ F. JANSSENS, *Bishop of Natches.*

"It is a very useful and practical work, and I trust it will have a wide circulation among Catholics."
✠ J. SWEENEY, *Bishop of St. John.*

"I consider it excellent in every way. It is interesting, instructive and edifying, and well calculated to do much good." ✠ JOHN WALSH, *Bishop of London, Ont.*

BENZIGER BROTHERS New York, Cincinnati and St. Louis.

THE YOUNG GIRL'S
BOOK OF PIETY
AT SCHOOL AND AT HOME.

A Prayer-Book for Girls in Convent-Schools and Academies,

BY

The Author of "Golden Sands."

TRANSLATED FROM THE 45th FRENCH EDITION.

Honored with a Blessing from the late POPE PIUS IX., and approved by many Archbishops and Bishops.

No.
4126, Cloth.. $ .80
4136, French morocco, gilt centre and edges........ 1.35
4136½, "   "   "   "   "   clasp........ 1.60
4147, Turkey morocco, antique, extra, gilt centre
    and edges...................................... 3.25
4147½, Turkey morocco, antique, extra, gilt centre
    and edges and clasp 3.75
4152, Calf, antique, edges red under gold.......... 3.50
4158, Silk velvet, rim and clasp, gilt edges, orn. centre 6.00
4161, "   "   "   "   "   rich ornaments 8.00

The Reverend author of this Prayer-book, for many years Spiritual Director of a Young Ladies' Academy, and who has devoted the best years of his life to the preparation of books of instruction for female youth, in this volume places his vast experience of human nature at the service of young girls in Convent-schools and Academies. The result is a book which embraces all that is essential for forming their tender hearts to piety and guiding their footsteps in the sure path of virtue. Written at the suggestion of a truly Christian heart, it breathes, from first to last, a perfume of sweet piety and of grace which often recalls the writings of St. Francis de Sales.

BENZIGER BROTHERS, New York, Cincinnati, and St. Louis.

Sent free by mail, on receipt of price.

THE IMITATION
OF THE
Sacred Heart of Jesus.

BY REV. F. ARNOUDT, S.J.

TRANSLATED FROM THE LATIN OF REV. J. M. FASTRE.

12mo, 798 pages, extra cloth, $2.00.

———o———

This delightful book contains ample matter for daily meditation throughout the year. The reader can start from the beginning and continue to the end of the work, or he may break this order and confine himself to such portions as are specially adapted to his feelings at the time. Things are not proposed here in general and in common, as is usually done in books of meditation, but everything is laid down specially and in particular, both in regard to the evil to be avoided, and the good to be practiced. The book greatly resembles the "Imitation of Christ," to which it is a fitting companion, but it is more regular in plan, more complete, actual, definite. The style of the work is everywhere suited to the subject, and the diction is pure

———o———

The Hidden Treasure;
OR, THE VALUE AND EXCELLENCE OF
THE HOLY MASS.
WITH A
Practical and Devout Method of Hearing it with Profit.

BY THE BLESSED LEONARD OF PORT-MAURICE.

18mo, 188 pages, cloth, 40 cents.

BENZIGER BROTHERS, New York, Cincinnati, and St. Louis.

Golden Sands.

THIRD SERIES.
TRANSLATED FROM THE FRENCH
By Miss ELLA McMAHON
32mo, cloth. 60 cents.

"I love these little messengers of God, one alone sometimes does more for me than a missionary."—Pius IX. to the Author of "Golden Sands."

"The practice of the little virtues, as St. Francis de Sales calls them, sanctifies daily life; and we know of no book, which insinuates these little virtues, more successfully than "Golden Sands."—*Ave Maria*.

"Rich in practical suggestions for the sanctification of daily duties."—*Catholic Mirror*.

"We hope the book will find its way into many Catholic houses and be the means of keeping the minds of Catholic children free from contamination of any kind."—*Connecticut Catholic*.

"Open the book anywhere, and you find a jewel of consolation, or explanation, or advice."—*Western Home Journal*.

"The work is small, but the beautiful counsels, and admonitions contained in it are great, and worthy of being stored in memory's store-house by every man, women, and child."—Pittsburg *Catholic*.

"Contains the very essence of the most profound thoughts told in the simplest and most charming style."—*Catholic Herald*.

"A collection of little counsels for the sanctification and happiness of daily life, and is a book which should be put in the hands of every young person."— New York *Sunday Union*.

"A book that can be opened at any page and read with profit. Its counsels heeded, would lead to happiness."—The Bay City, Mich., *Catholic Chronicle*.

"It is filled with good counsels, and no one can peruse it without benefit."—Richmond, Va., *Catholic Visitor*.

"Whatever may be one's failing or misery, strength and consolation can be found in the beautiful doctrines contained in this treasure."—Cleveland *Catholic Knight*.

BENZIGER BROTHERS, New York, Cincinnati, and St. Louis.

A BOOK FOR THE FAMILY!

GOFFINE'S
DEVOUT INSTRUCTIONS
ON THE EPISTLES AND GOSPELS.

For the Sundays and Holidays; with Explanations of Christian Faith and Duty and of Church Ceremonies. By the Rev. LEONARD GOFFINE. Translated by the Rev. THEO. NOETHEN.

Crown 8vo. Cloth, ink and gold side. Frontispiece. $1.50.

As a work of spiritual reading and instruction GOFFINE'S DEVOUT INSTRUCTIONS stands in the foremost rank. In it the faithful will find explained in a plain, simple manner the doctrines of the Church, her sacraments and ceremonies, as set forth in the Epistles and Gospels of the Sundays and holy days. The Catholic Church has at all times joined instruction with the offering of the Holy Sacrifice. But as the words of the speaker pass away and are forgotten, it is proper that preaching and spiritual reading should support each other. By this means instruction is more deeply impressed on the heart, and much that we might lose by neglect may thus be preserved. For these reasons, the reading of spiritual books is recommended as a means of properly keeping Sundays and holy days.

By the help of this book, those who are prevented by just cause from assisting at Mass may be enabled to arrange their family devotions. In Europe, the original of GOFFINE'S INSTRUCTIONS is extensively used for this purpose, and it is not only recommended and circulated there by the Bishops and priests, but some of the most learned and distinguished German divines have from time to time edited it.

The translator of the present Edition, which is undoubtedly **the best English version,** has not restricted himself to the text of any one Edition, but has made use of several of those that are most esteemed.

BENZIGER BROTHERS, New York, Cincinnati, and St. Louis.

GREETINGS
TO THE
CHRIST-CHILD.

A Collection of Christmas Poems for the Young.

EMBELLISHED WITH 89 ILLUSTRATIONS, TAILPIECES, ETC., ETC.

Square 16mo, on fine, super-calendered, tinted paper, full gilt back and gilt edges, elegant side stamp in gold, 50c.

BENZIGER BROTHERS, New York, Cincinnati, and St. Louis.

NEW PUBLICATIONS.

The Monk's Pardon.

A Historical Romance of the time of Philip IV. of Spain.

Translated from the French of RAOUL DE NAVÉRY

By ANNA T. SADLIER

12mo, cloth, $1.25.

This is one of the best works of perhaps the most popular Catholic novelist of France. The plot is strictly historical, the style pure, the interest admirably sustained and the moral excellent. It needs only to be known to acquire the popularity of the original, which has run through many editions in France.

Natalie Narischkin,

Sister of Charity of St. Vincent of Paul.

Translated from the French of Mme. AUGUSTUS CRAVEN,

By Lady GEORGIANA FULLERTON.

12mo, cloth, $1.00.

This book by the author of "A Sister's Story" is the biography of a noble Russian girl who becoming a Catholic, joined the Sisters of Charity, and devoted her life to working and suffering, as one Saint among a thousand others, in an institute where heroism is as common as the ordinary virtues are elsewhere, and sanctity is the universal rule. The narrative, enriched with copious extracts from her letters and numerous personal anecdotes, is interesting and edifying.

BENZIGER BROTHERS, New York, Cincinnati, and St. Louis.

NEW, ENLARGED EDITION.

Hours Before the Altar;
OR,
Meditations on the Holy Eucharist.

By MGR. DE LA BOUILLERIE,
Coadjutor Bishop of Bordeaux.

*Translated and Enlarged from the Fifty-First French Edition.
By a Sister of Mercy.*

32mo, Cloth, - - 50 Cents.

These meditations which have passed through fifty-one editions in France are addressed to those pious souls who have tasted the sweetness of the Lord in the Sacrament of the Altar. They are published in the hope that they will suggest a method of meditating on the sweet mystery of the Most Blessed Sacrament, and that they may prove like those feeble lamps suspended before our Sanctuaries, which give light enough to guide our steps to the Tabernacle, but not enough to diminish the charm of its mysterious darkness, coming thus as an aid to prayer, but without taking from its recollection.

A Thought of St. Teresa's
FOR EVERY DAY IN THE YEAR.

Translated from the French by Miss ELLA McMAHON.

32mo, Extra Cloth, 50 Cents.

This little book contains the **most precious thoughts** of one of the greatest mystic writers of the Church.

In it the pious soul will find prayerful suggestions, food for meditation, and consoling words in time of affliction. Short and to the point, these **thoughts** will be recurred to daily, and it is hoped may soon become familiar to the lips of American Catholics.

BENZIGER BROTHERS, New York, Cincinnati, and St. Louis.

My First Communion:
The Happiest Day of My Life.

A Preparation and Remembrance for First Communicants. Translated from the German of Rev. J. N. BUCHMANN, O.S.B., by Rev. RICHARD BRENNAN, LL.D.

With a Chromo-Frontispiece, and many full-page and other Illustrations. Extra cloth, 75 cents.

APPROBATIONS.

From the Right Rev. Bishop of Louisville.
" * * * It is a charming work, one of the best of its kind."

From Right Rev. Bishop of Erie.
" * * * Admirably calculated both in its style and the character of its contents to interest and instruct those for whom it is intended, the work should, and I hope will, receive a cordial welcome from parents, teachers, pastors, in fine all engaged in the training of youth."

From Right Rev. Bishop of Buffalo.
" * * * I believe that this 'delightfully interesting little volume will be welcomed *not only* by the children,' but by all good Pastors as well, to whom the first Communion of their children is one of the happiest and most important events of their holy ministry."

From Right Rev. Bishop of Providence.
" * * * I know no other book treating of the Most Holy Communion so well adapted to prepare children for that Sacrament and to leave wholesome, lasting impressions on their minds."

From Right Rev. Bishop of Ogdensburg.
"Your excellent book 'My First Communion,' I read with interest and edification."

From Right Rev. Bishop of Monterey and Los Angeles.
" * * * I heartily approve it and recommend it to our flock and Pastors."

From Right Rev. Vicar-Apostolic of Northern Minnesota.
"May this little book find a large circulation, and assist many to fervent and frequent Communions."

BENZIGER BROTHERS, New York, Cincinnati, and St. Louis.

THE LIFE OF
OUR LORD AND SAVIOUR JESUS CHRIST
AND OF HIS BLESSED MOTHER.

Translated and adapted from the original of Rev. L. C. BUSINGER,

By Rev. RICHARD BRENNAN, LL.D.,
Author of "A Popular Life of Pope Pius IX."

This is the first fully illustrated work on this subject ever published. It has nearly 600 Engravings in the body of the text, Chromo-Lithographs and Fine Plates; together with a superb Steel Engraving of "The Resurrection of Our Lord" (Size 20½x27 inches), which is

PRESENTED FREE

to every subscriber. The book is issued in 38 parts at

25 CENTS EACH,

and sold only by subscription.

BENZIGER BROTHERS, New York, Cincinnati, and St. Louis.

The Story of Jesus,

SIMPLY TOLD FOR THE YOUNG.

By ROSA MULHOLLAND.

With a preface by Rev. RICHARD BRENNAN, LL.D.

WITH 49 FULL-PAGE ILLUSTRATIONS AND 17 WOOD-CUTS IN THE TEXT.

Square 16mo, 172 pages, on fine, super-calendered, tinted paper, full gilt back, exquisite side-stamp in gold, extra cloth, 75c.

BENZIGER BROTHERS, New York, Cincinnati, and St. Louis.

SENT FREE BY MAIL, ON RECEIPT OF PRICE.

PEARLS FROM THE CASKET

OF THE

SACRED HEART OF JESUS.

A COLLECTION OF THE

Letters, Maxims, and Practices

OF THE

Blessed Margaret Mary Alacoque,

RELIGIOUS OF THE ORDER OF THE VISITATION.

EDITED BY

ELEANOR C. DONNELLY.

"I constitute thee heir of My Heart, and of all Its treasures for time and eternity, permitting thee to use them according to thy desire. I promise thee that thou shalt never want assistance until I shall fail in power. Thou shalt be forever Its beloved disciple, the delight of Its predilection, and the holocaust of Its love."—WORDS OF OUR LORD TO BLESSED MARGARET MARY.

32mo, 192 pages. Cloth, red edges, gilt side, 50 cents.

BENZIGER BROTHERS, New York, Cincinnati, and St. Louis.

THE LIFE AND ACTS
OF
POPE LEO THE THIRTEENTH.

Preceded by a Sketch of the Last Days of Pius the Ninth,
AND THE
ORIGIN AND LAWS OF THE CONCLAVE.

Compiled and translated from authentic sources. Edited by Rev. JOSEPH E. KELLER, S.J., President of St. Louis University, St. Louis.

Embellished with many beautiful Illustrations, Portraits, Views, etc., etc.

Published with the Approbation of His Eminence the Cardinal, Archbishop of New York.

Crown 8vo, 352 pages, extra cloth, bevelled boards, full gilt sides, $2.

Reliable Agents Wanted in all Parts of the Country.

BENZIGER BROTHERS, New York, Cincinnati, and St. Louis.

www.ingramcontent.com/pod-product-compliance
Lightning Source LLC
Chambersburg PA
CBHW031935230426
43672CB00010B/1929